Endorsements

Between their social image and pick-and-choose Christian belie
Steve and Barbara Uhlmann had actually managed to fool a
of people—primarily themselves. They had propped up a grand
illusion that they were living out a pretty decent love story when
all along it wasn't even close. When ghosts from their past finally
exposed how shallow their love actually was, it could have marked
the end of it all. Instead, it marked a new and wonderful beginning.
It took a lot of raw honesty and bare-knuckled forgiveness to get
there, but they found a love that few couples ever find. Fortunately,
their story shows all of us how we can find it too.

—Tim Kimmel, author of *Grace Based Parenting*

In a culture where relationships are falling apart, *Called 2 Love: The
Uhlmann Story* reminds us that it is never too late to build an amazing marriage.

—John Trent, PhD, The Gary Chapman Chair of Marriage and
Family Ministry and Therapy at Moody Theological Seminary

Every hour I invested in this book brought great delight! Steve's
and Barbara's insights into marriage and intimacy make me want
to stand up and cheer and tell everyone I know about this priceless
"work of heart"! No doubt it will have the same impact on all who
are open to learning what it means to recognize and minister to
your spouse's deepest needs.

—Shannon Ethridge, MA, life/relationship coach, speaker,
and author of twenty-two books, including the best-selling
Every Woman's Battle series

Called 2 Love: The Uhlmann Story is compelling, powerful, and needed. Steve and Barbara have done an incredible job of walking through real-life application of God's plan to heal and restore his people back into his image.

—Timothy R. Jennings, MD, author of *Could It Be This Simple?*,
The God-Shaped Heart, and *The God-Shaped Brain*

Called 2 Love: The Uhlmann Story is a heartfelt revelation told in a genuine attempt to help others make healthy change that brings about healing and true intimacy.

—Drs. Les and Leslie Parrott, authors of
Saving Your Marriage Before It Starts

This book provides a beautiful narrative of how transformational love can change the heart and make all the difference in a marriage.

—Darryl DelHousaye, DMin, Chancellor of Phoenix Seminary

Called 2 Love

The Uhlmann Story

A journey of self-discovery and joy-filled connection

Steve and Barbara Uhlmann

BroadStreet
PUBLISHING

BroadStreet Publishing® Group, LLC
Savage, Minnesota, USA
BroadStreetPublishing.com

Called 2 Love: The Uhlmann Story
A Journey of Self-Discovery and Joy-Filled Connection

978-1-4245-5921-3 (softcover)
978-1-4245-5922-0 (e-book)

Stock or custom editions of BroadStreet Publishing titles may be purchased in bulk for educational, business, ministry, fundraising, or sales promotional use. For information, please email info@broadstreetpublishing.com.

Cover and interior by Garborg Design at GarborgDesign.com.

Printed in the United States of America
20 21 22 23 24 5 4 3 2 1

Contents

1

Crisis on Aisle 9

"Steve ... I'm in real trouble." My voice was as shaky as my hands as I tried to speak coherently into my cell phone between wrenching gasps for breath. "This is Barbara ... I'm at Fry's Marketplace ... Come get me ... Quickly!"

My hands trembled so violently I could barely stuff my cellphone back into my purse. I was only a short distance from home, and I knew my husband would waste no time getting to me.

I had no idea what was happening. I didn't see it coming. I had no warning, no preliminary signs, no discomfort. Just minutes earlier, as I pushed my shopping cart casually through the Fry's Marketplace aisles, there was no way I could have known that, before I left that store, my life would change forever.

Nothing seemed wrong. Nothing was amiss. Why would it be? It was a beautiful summer day in Arizona. My husband and I had just returned from a delightful vacation, and I was on a routine trip to the store to pick up a few things to replenish our pantry. With no warning of impending disaster, I turned the corner from aisle 8 and entered aisle 9 to pick up a few frozen meats.

That's when it hit me.

I began to tremble violently. Sweat suddenly poured from my body like water from a compressed sponge, dripping from my head and drenching my summer clothes in seconds. A moment later my knees began to buckle. My breathing became labored, and I gasped for air as if I had just run a mile at full speed. I felt exhausted. My muscles seemed to turn to rubber, and I had to lean heavily on the cart to keep from collapsing. Wheezing audibly and shuffling because I could hardly lift my feet, I moaned, "Oh, Lord, what is happening to me? Please help me make it to the front of the store where someone will help me."

I managed to reach the checkout area, where shoppers didn't even seem to notice my distressed condition. No one offered help. I guess they didn't know what to do. I clung to the cart for dear life and dragged myself to a cushioned couch at the in-store Starbucks, where I collapsed, panting for breath. Still, no one came to my aid. One thought played over and over in my mind: Call Steve! Call Steve! I've got to call Steve!

I dug out my cellphone and aimed my shaking finger at Steve's number, hitting it after the third jab. The phone rang again and again. Oh, please pick up, Steve. Please! Three more rings and then his welcome voice said, "Hello." I managed to convey my distress, and he said, "I'll be right there."

Though it seemed like an hour, it was only minutes before I saw him burst through the door and look anxiously in all directions. When he spotted me—collapsed, shaking, and soaked as if doused by a bucket of water—his eyes widened in shock. He rushed over and lifted me to my feet, and I leaned heavily on his arm as he led me staggering to the car.

It was a five-minute drive to the nearest hospital, but Steve made it in two. He pulled up to the emergency room entrance, and immediately I was whisked away to face a battery of tests, leaving Steve in the waiting room with worry as his only companion.

What was happening to me? All kinds of grim scenarios paraded through my jumbled mind. Could I be having a heart attack? A stroke? Did I have an aneurysm? I had no idea. With nothing to do but allow myself to be probed, monitored, pushed through pulsating machines, and scanned by X-rays, I imagined the worst. I felt powerless—a feeling that increased with each passing moment.

After three hours of tests, questions, and examinations, the doctor finally came to Steve and me with the results. I braced myself for the worst.

"We think you have suffered a panic attack."

I stared at him for a long moment, unable to process the diagnosis.

Steve, who was at my side, jumped in. "What's a panic attack?" He seemed relieved that it wasn't a heart attack, but still puzzled.

"A panic attack," the doctor said, "is a sudden episode of intense fear that triggers severe physical reactions even though there is no real danger."

That explanation didn't help. I couldn't remember feeling any fear.

Steve looked at me and asked, "What would cause you to have a panic attack?"

"I have no idea," I replied. I could not wrap my mind around a traumatic event so physically real being triggered by some nonexistent danger. What did I have to be afraid of? How could the placid, benign frozen-food section of a grocery store bring on such devastating symptoms?

None of this made sense to me or Steve. If anything, I should have been more relaxed and happier than ever. We had just returned from the best vacation we had ever experienced. Steve had sold our highly successful business a few years earlier, which allowed him to retire early. We now had the time and funds to fulfill our dreams and live happily ever after. We were supposed to be having the time of our lives.

We had spent three weeks on Maui, one of our favorite places in the world. Then after a brief stop at home, we flew overseas for another three weeks, including a two-week Holy Land tour. Those six weeks of seeing new things, visiting extensively with old friends, and spending time with each other had been rejuvenating and invigorating, both individually and for us as a couple.

Now, just twenty-four hours after returning home, I was in the ER with a doctor telling me I was reacting violently to some intense, violent fear of something that didn't physically exist. Neither Steve nor I could understand it. We asked for more details.

When the doctor put the diagnosis in clinical terms, it confused me even more. He said I had adrenal stress disorder, chronic fatigue syndrome, and PTSD (post-traumatic stress disorder).

"PTSD?" Steve repeated, incredulous. "Isn't that what affects soldiers returning home from horrific war experiences? How could my wife have PTSD? She's never been in the military, much less in a war."

"No, of course she hasn't," he replied. "But PTSD is not necessarily related specifically to battle trauma. It affects more people than just soldiers. Anyone who has faced traumatic events in the past can have it, and the symptoms can remain hidden for years, then burst out at unexpected times."

"Well, whatever caused my attack," I said, "it happened, and it's over now. So I guess I'm in the clear."

"No, that's not the way it works," the doctor responded. "Your stress trigger needs to be identified and dealt with. If you ignore it, attacks like you had today will almost certainly continue."

I still couldn't understand why I would have PTSD. What kind of traumatic stress could I be reacting to? Where was all this coming from, and what could I do about it? Steve took me home. I was in too much of a fog to even think clearly, but Steve did enough worrying for both of us. While I began several months of rest, the engineer in Steve took over. He was driven to understand what had happened to me, so as soon as I was settled, he was on the Internet to learn all he could about this confusing diagnosis, while I began months of rest.

After searching numerous websites, Steve learned that the adrenal glands are the stress managers of the body. Their basic function is to control how we respond to stress. For example, if I were confronted with an external threat, such as being chased by a bear, a chain reaction would be set in motion. My entire nervous system would go into high alert. I would breathe faster. My heart rate would increase. Adrenaline would kick in. Blood vessels in my torso would restrict and push blood toward my arms and legs to give me the extra boost I needed to outrun the bear.

According to The National Institute of Mental Health of Bethesda, Maryland, "It is natural to feel afraid during and after a traumatic situation. Fear triggers many split-second changes in the body to help defend against danger or to avoid it. This 'fight-or-flight' response is a physical reaction meant to protect a person from harm."[1] This heightened alert state lasts as long as the danger is present. Once we are safe again, the body is supposed to revert to its normal state.

What can happen, however, is this: If we experience trauma of some kind and fail to address it adequately, especially in childhood, the brain will store the memory, often burying it deep in the subconscious mind. But because the traumatic event has not been resolved, certain situations will trigger the brain to act as though the threat is still present. The actual threat has passed, but our subconscious mind still perceives the danger as a threat even though it has been emotionally buried.

Steve learned that the problem with burying unresolved traumas of the past is that they don't stay buried. Sooner or later they resurrect themselves in unhealthy ways. I may have suppressed or buried some past hurts and fears, but I buried them alive. The frightening or hurtful experience may be buried, but because it has not been resolved, it continually pushes to get out. The brain doesn't want to face the emotional pain again, so it submerges the memory deep within the subconscious mind to prevent it from coming to the surface and forcing the conscious mind to relive the pain caused by the experience.

A battle to repress the traumatic memory rages deep within, and a person may not even be aware of it. But over time, the buried pain builds up so much emotional pressure that it can no longer be contained. Like an overheated engine bursting a water hose, the unhealed hurt spews out in the form of various symptoms. Those symptoms can include bad dreams, frightening thoughts, feeling tense or on edge, sleeping difficulties, angry outbursts, negative thoughts about oneself, avoiding contact with people, and secluding oneself.[2]

A trauma that hasn't been dealt with can also trigger an extreme physical reaction, as it did to me in aisle 9 at Fry's. The body somehow detects that something is wrong even though the danger cannot be consciously identified. The result can be a toxic buildup that overloads and eventually compromises the immune system. That leaves the body susceptible to all kinds of physical problems. That, apparently, was the case with me.

It is not uncommon for severe symptoms of buried hurts to be delayed for months or even years after the traumatic event occurs. That means buried, unhealed hurts will remain a problem until they are deliberately dug out and brought to the surface for healing.

What was my buried trauma? That was what I could not figure out. I led what many would consider the ideal life. I had a loving, hard-working husband and two lovely daughters. We had no financial problems. I watched my diet and exercised daily. I was involved in many church activities and ministries—a walking example of the perfect church lady. So what was this hidden problem that suddenly thrust its ugly, unwelcome face into my life?

While I was growing up, I don't remember anyone ever telling me that suppressing hurts or feelings was a bad thing. In fact, I was encouraged to suppress them. Yet now it seemed I was being put on notice that somewhere along the way I had buried a severe hurt and if it was not unearthed and healed, it would act like a scabbed-over infection and cause real problems. My body had sounded a warning through the adrenal stress disorder and chronic fatigue syndrome. These outward physical signs were a way of getting my attention to tell me I needed to deal with the inward me. Indeed, they did get my attention, and Steve's as well.

As I thought about it, I realized that I may have had warnings that this freight train had been barreling down the track toward me for some time. When Steve and I took our Holy Land tour just prior to my attack, my mind had begun to take on a negative, uneasy sensation as the tour guide led us through a museum filled with ancient Scripture manuscripts. Beautiful as the manuscripts were, I thought they looked fragile, worn, and tired, long exposed to the ravages of use and time. They were in grave need of protection and tender loving care. That's why they were under glass in a climate-controlled museum. At that moment, I felt like those manuscripts. I was tired, my feet hurt, and I needed to sit for a while. The tour could go on without me for now.

Steve had just left the group a couple of minutes earlier. He had seen a place where he could buy a Diet Coke, and he set out to satisfy his thirst, intending to catch up with us later.

I headed in the direction he had gone, hoping to find a place to sit. I was not concerned about anything except my aching feet—until I got to the place where I was sure Steve would be and found that he wasn't there. Suddenly I felt a twisting sensation in my stomach. I looked around every corner, down every corridor, but I saw no sign of him.

I knew he couldn't have gone far. Logically, I understood I was in no danger. I thought, *as soon as Steve realizes I'm not with the group, he'll immediately come find me.* Yet my logic began to be supplanted by an emerging dread, fueled by weariness and aching feet. I began to feel alone and helpless. I started to cry. This is typical of Steve, I thought, just to disappear without warning, without regard to my feelings, following whatever shiny object catches his attention. I began to feel panicky. I was alone in a foreign country, and he was nowhere to be seen.

I need not have worried, of course. Steve did miss me and set out to search for me. He found me quickly, before the seeds of my anxiety sprouted into a full-blown attack.

Had I been honest with myself and explored my feelings a bit further, I would have realized that I often had moments of this kind of budding anxiety in my everyday life. I would feel stabs of fear when there was no visible threat, and I had been developing sleep problems.

Looking back at these events, I can see that the PTSD did not just appear out of nowhere. It had given warning signs of its approach like the distant rumble of thunder presages a full-blown storm. But I could not figure out what the source of my problem might be, so Steve and I remained perplexed by the whole experience, mainly because we had not connected the dots. We couldn't imagine that I had buried any kind of pain or trauma that could affect me so dramatically.

In the following days, things seemed to return to normal, and our fears began to dissipate. "You know, Steve," I said one day, "I think whatever it was in my past that caused the panic attack must have been released in the attack itself. That hidden incident just needed to boil over and explode. It did that at Fry's Marketplace, and that's that. It's all over, and we need not worry about it anymore."

"I've been thinking the same thing," Steve agreed. "Things are now back to normal, and we can get on with our travels. The more we worry about it, the worse it will become."

Or so we thought. But my body didn't get the message.

A few days later, I was upstairs in our two-story home. I wasn't doing anything strenuous or thinking anything stressful. Nothing was on my mind that should have triggered another attack. But suddenly I found myself on the floor, flat on my back. I couldn't move. At that moment even lifting my head was impossible. My body felt like it weighed four hundred pounds.

I tried to roll over so I could at least crawl to a phone and call for help, but the best I could do was curl up in a fetal position. I couldn't even raise my hand. It seemed as though my body had gone on strike, refusing to follow orders from my brain.

In the grocery store, I had been unable to control the shaking, but at least I could move my feet well enough to shuffle along. This time I couldn't even do that. My body was in complete rebellion, as though to say, "You don't like shaking? Well then, we won't move at all. We'll just lie here. See how you like that!" I knew Steve was on his way home, so I quit struggling and lay there crying as I waited for him.

It seemed that I had lain there for hours, though it was really only about fifteen minutes before I heard Steve walk into the house. When he got halfway up the stairs he could hear me crying, and his pace quickened as he hurried to my side.

"Barbara, what in the world has happened?" he cried as he helped me sit up.

"I—I don't really know. I think I fell … or … or … collapsed. At least, I was standing and feeling okay, then I was on the floor. Felt heavy … Couldn't get up … Couldn't move at all. I was so scared." I started crying again.

Steve brought me a sandwich and something to drink as he tried to soothe me. "Okay, okay, it's all right now. Everything's going to be fine. Apparently, you have issues we've got to deal with. We'll figure this out and get to the bottom of it. Just relax for now."

I could tell by Steve's tone that he was frustrated. He had plans for us—travel, ministries, projects—and my persistent problem seemed likely to throw a wrench into the gears. He wanted to fix things—to fix me, that is—so we could get on with our plans.

When I finished my sandwich, I said, "I'm sorry, Steve. I don't want my problem to cause us to miss out on—"

"It need not cause us to miss out on anything," he interrupted. "I'll just get someone who's qualified to help you get beyond whatever this thing is that's messing up your life."

"I just don't get it," I said. "If I don't know what childhood traumas are affecting me now as an adult, what am I supposed to do? How can I deal with them?"

"It doesn't make sense to me either," Steve agreed.

Despite our doubts and confusion, medical professionals insisted that some buried trauma in my past was causing my present health crisis. And if my past was affecting my present, then it wasn't really in the past—it had broken out of the past and invaded the present. It was somehow with me right now, intruding into my life and causing me great distress.

I had no idea what it was, but I knew I must begin my search for the offending culprit.

2

In Search of the Real Barbara

That second panic attack left me with several ongoing issues, including back pain, low blood sugar, low blood pressure, chronic fatigue, and foggy thinking. But to me, the worst problem was my inability to sleep.

After that second attack, Steve insisted that I not be left alone, even for an hour or two. We recruited the help of a young woman I know who is a trained caregiver. When this caregiver was off duty, Steve made sure I had someone on hand to help me physically whenever it was needed. He usually hired women from an agency.

Whatever the problem was, it clearly wasn't rooted in my present life, or at least it didn't seem to be. The problem couldn't be in my marriage. Steve and I got along wonderfully. I loved him and he loved me. The problem couldn't be financial worries. Steve's sale of his business had left us well positioned financially. The problem couldn't be any unmet physical needs. I had everything I needed physically. We lived in a lovely home, had plenty to eat, had good health (up to now), and all such needs were met. The problem couldn't be in my spiritual life. I knew Jesus personally and had followed him faithfully since my conversion at age fourteen. By all appearances I was living a wonderful life.

To help me get to the bottom of things, Steve called a family friend, Linda Milner, a highly successful certified life coach. It was the best thing we ever did throughout the entire ordeal. She came to our house almost daily to walk me through a recovery process, becoming my guide to help me deal with whatever was causing my problem.

To know Linda is to love her. Imagine a petite bundle of wiry-blonde energy, with wide eyes that are kind yet piercing. She bubbles with wit and humor, and is blessed with an infectious laugh at anything funny that inevitably draws you to join the merriment. While tender and caring when it's called for, she is also tough, no-nonsense, and unbending as an oak tree when necessary.

Before I tell you how Linda began working with me, it will give you some insight into what follows if I back up and explain some of my earlier contacts with her. She knew from the beginning that I was as emotionally "frozen"—to use her word—as I could be. One of our first interactions came in Steve's office where we talked about our past. I had very limited memory of my childhood, especially of my dad, and Linda met with me alone a couple of times to explore that, without much success. I remembered that he and my mom divorced, that he was a really nice guy, and that we went to see him every summer. That was about it.

But that was not the end of Linda's probing. Sometime later, a friend invited me to attend one of Linda's professional retreats and one of the goals of the retreat was to help women get in touch with their past and draw out any buried, unhealed emotions that might be disrupting their present lives.

Near the end of the retreat, we did a visualization exercise. We all sat in a circle with music playing in the background, low enough that we could hear Linda but loud enough that we couldn't hear each other. She handed each of us a pillow to use, in case we needed to cry into it or to muffle something we said that we didn't want anyone else to know. Presumably we could also punch it if we felt the need.

"I'm going to describe some pictures," Linda began, "and I want you to visualize them. They will bring up memories from your past that you may have forgotten."

The goal was to evoke emotions linked to the pictures. The visualized images, the music in the background, and the memories worked together to activate all the senses simultaneously. Linda wanted us to get painful memories out in the open.

We closed our eyes and she started describing a scene as we tried to visualize ourselves walking through an area, looking at the things she designated. She described vignettes that seemed almost random, though they weren't. She described old dusty pictures or a pile of junk sitting to one side of our path. As she spoke, our minds filled in the details, and the dusty pictures became old family photos. The junk piles transformed into images of old toys and childhood treasures and they conjured memories of events and the people associated with them.

At least that's how it seemed to work for everyone else in the room. Unintelligible murmuring by voices hidden in the pillows surrounded me as Linda encouraged us to give voice to what we were feeling, to say what we had always wanted to say and never could. Linda walked around the circle, whispering in our ears, "Tell them how they hurt you. Tell them how angry you are. Tell them how you feel. Tell them!" In a short time the voices gave way to crying.

Except for me. I wasn't feeling anything. I dutifully buried my face in the pillow and went through the motions, mustering up the best display of emotion I could. Anything to get this exercise over with. I hadn't really wanted to come on the retreat in the first place.

The recorded music finally came to an end, but instead of moving on, Linda started it over again. And when it ran out a second time, she started it for a third round. She told me later that she knew I was faking it. And she wasn't about to let me get away with it. Years of working with all kinds of people had made her very perceptive. The other women had broken through to deep emotions, but she would not be satisfied until I joined them. She could tell that I wasn't hiding my feelings; I just didn't have access to them.

Then something remarkable started to happen. Long forgotten memories started to creep in and as they did, I started to ... feel. I broke and suddenly real tears poured out. It was painful, yet it felt wonderful at the same time. The euphoria of that experience went with me for a time after that retreat, but as often happens I gradually fell back into the same old habit patterns and closed up again.

No doubt this prior knowledge of my emotional repression shaped the hardline approach Linda took with me from the beginning.

I'll never forget the first day Linda came into our living room to begin her duties. She sat down with a notepad on her lap and a pen in her hand. After a bit of obligatory small talk, she looked me in the face and said, "Barbara, I want you to cancel all your appointments. Let me see your calendar."

I glared at her in disbelief. "You've got to be kidding. You know I can't do that. I do work at the church. I help run a women's ministry. I work on retreats. You can't expect me to turn my back on all that."

"Yes, I do expect it. You are much too busy. Frankly, I think you ought to be in the hospital. But since you're not, I'm taking over your life like a pirate commandeering a ship. You are going to cancel those appointments. You don't understand how sick you are."

"Well, maybe I'll cancel a few of them, but some people are counting on me. I simply can't abandon them."

"Yes, you can. And you will," Linda said. "You can't get well with these distractions pulling you in fifty different directions. As much as you hate to do it, we've got to focus your full attention on yourself until we get this problem solved."

"But, Linda—"

"Don't you 'but Linda' me. Now, hand over your calendar."

Reluctantly, I gave her my daily planner.

You cannot imagine how hard this hit me. My calendar was my life. My church work was what I lived for. But Linda would not relent or even compromise, so I canceled all my precious appointments and became an alien to my calendar.

I felt lost, naked, floating in a void, drifting without an anchor. This is exactly what Linda needed me to feel in order to work with me. For the next several months, she would be my anchor.

I remained under a doctor's care to address the physical problems that plagued me after the panic attacks, particularly the chronic fatigue syndrome. A specialist in Florida brought that problem under partial control with medication and supplements. Sleep remained a problem, however, and I soon found it necessary to depend on nonaddictive prescriptions to help me sleep and a mild sedative to ward off recurring bouts with fear and anxiety.

But dealing with the emotional side of my issues presented a greater challenge. Much greater. Linda knew the key to my wholeness was hidden somewhere in my past, and she was determined to dig that out of me—to bring whatever hurt was buried there into the open to be aired out. We settled into a comfortable sofa in the living room, and she began to probe much as you would expect.

"Barbara, I want you to take yourself back into your past—particularly to your childhood. Tell me about your growing-up years."

"Well, there was my parent's divorce," I said.

"How old were you when they divorced?"

"Nine."

"Did you have brothers or sisters?"

"Yes, a sister one year older and a younger brother."

"Did you get along well with your siblings?"

"Yes. With Rob being a boy and considerably younger, we didn't have that much in common. But Mary Ann and I got along superbly, even though our temperaments were quite different. She had a mind of her own, which meant she was often rebellious with my mom. She always wanted her own way. But with me she was a good companion and a lot of fun."

"How about you? Were you also rebellious?"

"Oh no, not at all. I always tried to be a good, obedient daughter."

"Did you resent your sister's rebellion?" she asked. "Did you feel a desire to do things your own way like she did instead of being so obedient all the time?"

"No, I don't remember ever feeling anything like that. I liked being obedient. It kept things smooth and on an even keel."

"How about your parents? What was their marriage like?"

"I don't remember much about their marriage. I just know they had to divorce."

"That must have really hurt you." Linda looked at me, and her focus became more intense. I could tell that she thought she might have found a key to my childhood pain. "So how did you feel about that?"

"I don't think I felt anything in particular. I guess I was too young. I didn't think it was any big deal."

At that point, Linda paused and looked out the window, absently tapping her pencil on her notepad. Finally, she looked at me and said, "There are some painful experiences back there somewhere. We've just got to find them. You seem to have built a barrier between the hurt you experienced in the past and the person you have become in the present. We need to get in touch with the real you, and that includes visiting your past, even if it hurts a little to discuss it."

"But I don't know how to break those barriers or find those hurts," I said. "I'm just not aware of anything like that in my past."

"Well, I think it's there," Linda replied. "Somewhere closed away in a deep, dark corner inside you is probably a little girl—the little girl you used to be—who is harboring some painful hurts that you have never acknowledged. They are probably hurts you don't want to face again. That's why you have closed them off, locked them up, and thrown away the key. Somehow, we've got to get you in touch with that little girl who experienced those hurts."

In saying this, Linda was not merely shooting in the dark or groping blindly for a solution. She told me later that I had already revealed a clue that gave her insight into my hurt. That clue was my desire to please people. I had gone to the women's group session because I had wanted to please the person inviting me. I had faked crying into the pillow because I wanted to please Linda. She had seen evidence that I acquiesced to Steve's wishes because I wanted to please him. She had seen me take on church tasks because I wanted to please others. She knew those people-pleasing incidents were all clues that indicated a strong fear of rejection—that I was afraid people would not accept me for who I am, so I reached out for acceptance by doing things to please them.

It really seemed strange to me. I had apparently buried my childhood hurts so deep that I couldn't feel them anymore. Yet at the same time, those hurts had apparently shaped the way I lived my life. The more I realized how traumatic that hurt must have been to affect my life so deeply, the more I found myself dreadfully frightened at the prospect of uncovering whatever lay buried down there.

Linda explained that hurts are an inevitable part of living. The only way to live without pain is to close oneself off to the possibility of hurt, and the only way to do that is to close oneself off to relationships and to love. To be an authentic, feeling person means opening up oneself to relationships, which always leaves one vulnerable to being hurt. Facing my fears and hurts was a process I must go through to become an authentic, loving, and feeling person. It would be painful, but she assured me it would be worth it to connect with my wounded inner self, find healing, and become real.

To open my mind to these unfamiliar concepts, Linda gave me a list of several books to read. Among these was *The Velveteen Rabbit* by Margery Williams, a children's classic published in 1922. This book touched me deeply. It's a story about a stuffed toy rabbit made of velveteen that's given to a young boy as a Christmas present. But the boy disdains the old-fashioned stuffed animal, preferring instead to play with his more modern mechanical toys. The wisest and oldest toy in the nursery is the Skin Horse. He tells Rabbit about toys that have magically become real. Rabbit is fascinated with the idea of becoming real and asks the Skin Horse to tell him how that happens:

> "Real isn't how you were made," said the Skin Horse. "It's a thing that happens to you. When a child loves you for a long, long time, not just to play with you, but REALLY loves you, then you become Real."
> "Does it hurt?" asked Rabbit.
> "Sometimes," said the Skin Horse, for he was always truthful. "When you are real you don't mind being hurt."[3]

Those words touched me in an unexpected way, and I actually cried as I read them. I suddenly realized how much I wanted to be real and authentic. Linda was right. From childhood and on into my adult life, I was always trying to please others in order to feel accepted and loved. Subconsciously I was afraid to reveal my real feelings—my real wants, needs, and fears. It seemed I was convinced that people would not accept and love the real me, so I naturally tried my best to be what I thought others wanted me to be.

You would think pleasing people would be fulfilling, but it wasn't. To the contrary, it was exhausting to always be doing what I thought others expected. People offered me plenty of gratitude and thanks for my efforts, but a persistent sense of unworthiness kept me from receiving that their appreciation and acceptance was meant for the real me. Down deep I was convinced that they appreciated and accepted only what I did for them. They would want me around only as long as I continued to please them. Emotionally I thought it was my activity that was being accepted rather than the real me. I was not sure I knew who the real me was, which meant I had little hope of finding her.

For Rabbit, there didn't seem to be much hope either. The mechanical toys seemed much more valuable because they did all kinds of tricks that he couldn't do. He was just a floppy old stuffed rabbit. What value could he have that anyone would want?

Then one night the boy couldn't find his favorite toy—the one he always took to bed. In its place, his nana gave him Rabbit to sleep with. Suddenly the boy became enamored with this soft stuffed rabbit that was so huggable. At first, Rabbit found all the attention a little uncomfortable. He was squeezed tightly, stroked a lot, and sometimes the boy even rolled over on him in bed. In addition, he was dragged everywhere the boy went.

> But very soon he grew to like it, for the Boy
> used to talk to him, and made nice tunnels
> for him under the bedclothes that he said
> were like burrows that real rabbits lived in.[4]

One day the boy came down with scarlet fever. The doctor ordered that he be taken to the seaside. Because of the severity of the disease, his room was to be disinfected. This included burning all his books and toys.

Rabbit, along with the other items from the boy's room, was removed that night to the garden to be burned the next morning. Rabbit painfully reflected on his life with the boy. Feeling abandoned and alone, he shed a real tear. When the tear dropped to the ground, a flower magically appeared. A fairy emerged from the flower and, through her magic, turned the Velveteen Rabbit into a real rabbit.

> "Wasn't I Real before?" asked the little
> Rabbit.
> "You were Real to the Boy," the Fairy
> said, "because he loved you. Now you
> shall be Real to everyone."[5]

When Rabbit shed that tear at being left alone, I also wept. Why did I feel his aloneness so deeply? Where was that feeling coming from? I wasn't sure. Yet the feeling emerged and persisted, drawn out of me by the story. I realized that this strong feeling of empathy with the Rabbit could not have arisen had it not been present somewhere within me. It must have emerged from something I felt deeply as a child—something akin to what the Rabbit felt.

God used *The Velveteen Rabbit* to open a door just a crack, enabling me to feel a sliver of what the little girl I was years ago must have felt. I wanted to reach inside and release that memory so I could be real to everyone. I sensed that hidden somewhere deep inside me was a real Barbara, but I couldn't quite reach her. I vaguely sensed her presence, but she remained invisible to me and to everyone else.

Of course, my friends and family were all aware of a Barbara. This Barbara was always smiling and doing what others wanted done and saying what others wanted to hear. But she was coming to realize that her continued attempt to meet the needs of others, which is in essence a good thing, was coming from a sense of unworthiness, causing her to hide the truth about who she really is, which is not a good thing.

I was starting to realize that when I buried the hurts of my childhood, I buried the real me with them. The real me who could feel and speak up and express what I felt and wanted and dreamed of was buried so deep that I couldn't touch her. I could barely sense that she was even there. But reading that simple children's book ignited within me a desire to be a real person, which was the desire that eventually brought real personhood to the Velveteen Rabbit.

Who was this person hiding deeply within, desperately gripping all those painful memories and refusing to let them go? How could I get to know that real me hiding inside? And if I did find her, would I like what I discovered?

I was about to find out.

3

What Real Emotions Feel Like

The Velveteen Rabbit opened the door to my past just a crack—barely enough to give me a vague, disquieting taste of the feelings of loneliness and fear I had experienced somewhere in my childhood, but not enough to identify the source of those feelings. Obviously, it was a door shut tight and locked down, and the watchdogs of my subconscious guarded it with bared fangs to prevent that deep childhood pain from ever assailing my conscious mind again.

The doctors and Linda insisted that I needed to identify and face that childhood pain, which to me was a terrifying prospect that I resisted with all my might. But Linda overrode my protests and guided me in the process. She pointed out what the apostle Paul had to say about how we deal with our childhood. He wrote, "When I was a child, I talked like a child, I thought like a child, I reasoned like a child. When I became a man, I put the ways of childhood behind me" (1 Corinthians 13:11 NIV). In other words, he grew up and became an adult. That's what becoming mature spiritually and emotionally is all about.

Paul went on to write, "We will be mature in the Lord, measuring up to the full and complete standard of Christ. Then we will no longer be immature like children" (Ephesians 4:13–14 NLT). The meaning was clear to me. If I wanted to mature into the me I was intended to be, I must uncover and through healing put away that childhood trauma that I insisted on ignoring.

At first, Steve had trouble grasping the concepts that Linda was introducing to me. He thought it was strange that I needed to visit my childhood pain to connect with myself. "Why can't you just leave whatever is in your past in the past?" he asked. One day he blurted out, "When I hear you referring to your childlike Barbara in the third person, it sort of freaks me out. I mean, how does conversing with yourself as if you were two people bring you to maturity?" But Steve wanted me to get to the bottom of my problem (actually, he was hoping Linda would "fix" me emotionally) and he said, "If it means a little self-talk to get you there, then by all means, go for it."

Of course, I had physically grown up and become a mature woman, which meant that judging by all appearances, I had "put the ways of childhood behind me." But there was apparently one aspect of my childhood emotions that had not been allowed to grow. It was stuck, and that crucial part of me had not moved past some obstacle that had blocked my healthy progress toward emotional and relational maturity. Linda showed me that I must return to that emotional place in my childhood, find the little girl I was then, and free her from the binding trauma of her fear and pain. Only then would I be able to move into real, unencumbered personhood, free of fear, free of pain, and free to give and receive love fully.

By now I could see the value of the path Linda was setting me on, but fear still held me back. If I did get in touch with the childlike Barbara, what would I discover? Could I bear to face again whatever pain had shut her down and caused her to hide the real me? You wouldn't think the process would be that scary, but it was. What if I found within myself feelings of insecurity, betrayal, or resentment toward Steve? What would happen when he learned of those feelings? He would surely be upset—maybe so upset he would leave me. That would hurt beyond what I could bear.

Or, if in uncovering the childlike Barbara, I found that I was a different person from the one those around me knew, would they accept the new me? I did not feel that I had a truly safe place to be real—to reveal the person I really am and expect love and acceptance despite what flaws and inadequacies might be lurking within my real self. I vacillated. Maybe this quest to become real wasn't worth the risk.

Linda used Scripture to push me off high center. She showed me that God loves me for who I am and that he is a safe place to be real. She assured me that I could safely share with him what I was afraid to reveal. She read to me 1 Peter 5:7, urging me to "cast all your anxiety on him because he cares for you" (NIV). She pulled out many verses from the

Psalms, such as Psalm 46:1: "God is our refuge and strength, always ready to help in times of trouble."

Perhaps the Scripture that touched me most deeply at the time was Isaiah 45:3, which says, "I will give you treasures hidden in the darkness—secret riches. I will do this so you may know that I am the Lord." I sensed that this treasure hidden in the darkness was the real me, locked away in the depths of my very being. God wanted me to discover that treasure. Those "secret riches" were the reality of who I really am—the person who had been kept in hiding since childhood.

I struggled to find the will to open myself to God. I knew in my mind that he was a safe place to share my hurts—the one I could trust and tell what I had experienced in my childhood and what that felt like. He would take the wounded childlike Barbara in his arms and bless her as a beautiful child of God.

I realized that if I was ever to find healing and to know and love myself as a person of intrinsic value, I had to get in touch with that wounded little girl I used to be, learn what had destroyed her sense of worth, and present her to the loving arms of Jesus, where she could find healing and become unstuck. Then she could be free to be real.

When I worked up the courage to take whatever steps were necessary to find what was hidden inside me, Linda was ready with a plan. She suggested something that really seemed odd to me at first.

"Here is what I want you to do," she said. "I want you to begin keeping a daily journal that describes both what you experience day by day in the present and what you remember from your past. Go back into your childhood and pull up what you can remember when you were just a little girl. When you think of those memories, write what you feel about them."

"Okay, that seems easy enough," I replied.

"Now, here's the trick," she went on. "When you describe those feelings you had as a child, write them down with your left hand."

"But I'm right-handed," I protested.

"I know. But let your left hand express your childlike voice and your right hand express your adult voice. Try it."

"Doesn't that seem a little contrived? A little like a game or a trick?"

"Just humor me, Barbara."

I was skeptical at first. But I soon found that writing out the feelings about my childhood memories with my left hand had a strange, even almost eerie, effect. By changing hands, I was somehow able to engage my memories differently. My left handwriting was cramped and unsteady; it looked much like the scrawl of a child. The very awkwardness of the process and the cramped visual results began to make me feel that when I wrote with my left hand, I became a little girl again. It enabled me to place myself in the past and to see things through the eyes of that little girl I was at the age of eight or nine. The real goal of the procedure, of course, was to help me uncover emotions I had buried during those years. To give a voice to whatever pain and frustrations I had felt. No emotions were to be off-limits and no frustrations ignored.

My initial problem was that I had kept emotions at bay for so long that I didn't even know how to identify them. I was not sure what real emotions felt like. To help me identify my feelings, Linda gave me a list of just about every emotion any human being has ever felt. When I sat down to write about any particular event I remembered, I scanned the list to find the words that expressed my feelings about it. Here's the list:

Feelings[6]

Angry	Nervous	Depressed	Terrified
Furious	Jittery	Unimportant	Frightened
Antagonistic	Exasperated	Belittled	Suffocated
Resentful	Irritable	Confused	Trapped
Spiteful	Bewildered	Mixed-up	Lost
Vengeful	Bored	Out-of-it	Uptight
Bitter	Oppressed	Cherished	Suicidal
Tricked	Burdened	Desirable	Ugly
Deceived	Sad	Free	Picked-on
Ticked-off	Lonely	Attractive	Harassed
Insecure	Dumb	Jolly	Wary
Inadequate	Foolish	Forgiven	Shy
Useless	Cheated	Carefree	Worried
Violated	Old	Generous	Tense
Haughty	Talkative	Compassionate	Arrogant
Pitied	Helpless	Anxious	Cowardly
Weary	Hurt	Loved	Uncomfortable
Wrung-out	Happy	Awed	Rejected
Tired	Joyful	Humble	Unwanted
Humiliated	Excited	Bold	Disgusted
Small	Magnanimous	Hopeful	Frustrated
Insulted	Grateful	Fit	Guilty
Restless	Confident	Lighthearted	Embarrassed
Jumpy	Accepted	Disappointed	Unfulfilled
Betrayed	Worthwhile	Afraid	Empty
Aloof	Important	Apprehensive	Overwhelmed

Looking at this extensive list of emotions, I can guess that some readers will suspect that the list became the tail that wagged the dog. I came into the process with no identifiable feelings, so these words became suggestive and enabled me to name feelings I might not have really felt. To put it another way, some might think the list allowed me to artificially conjure up a feeling based solely on what a given word suggested. I suppose that could have been the case at first—I'm not sure. But I can assure you that as I got into the process, these words became merely prime for the pump. The emotions were deep and buried, and the words I found to identify them woke them up and pulled them to the surface like Jesus calling Lazarus from the grave.

As I began to get in touch with the child I was in the past, I (the adult Barbara) began to communicate with her and she with me as if we were separate entities. Please understand that I was under no illusion that she was actually a separate person from me. I knew that treating her as such was a sort of self-imposed fiction that gave me a more realistic perspective on my feelings. I fully realized that when the childlike Barbara expressed a feeling, it was really my own feeling she expressed and not the feeling of an entity separate from me.

In my earliest journal communications with the childlike Barbara, I often asked her how she felt. Here is one of her earliest emotional responses:

> Frightened, unwanted, trapped,
> unimportant, insecure, afraid, sad, helpless.

It seemed that the childlike Barbara was hiding, huddled in a corner, confined within an enclosed space and locked securely behind a heavy door. But at least she was now communicating, and that was encouraging.

As the process began to work, it became a little scary, like venturing alone into a haunted house on a moonless night. Childlike Barbara began to reveal memories that had lain dormant for years. At first it was not too bad. Those earliest memories emerged from the home where we lived in Denver, Colorado. (I was born in Washington, DC, where my parents lived while my father attended medical school on the GI bill. Then we moved to Denver, where he completed his residency to become a doctor.)

I have a photo of our complete family—Dad, Mom, Mary Ann, Rob, and me—taken when we lived in Denver. In that picture we look like a normal, happy family. Gazing at it took me back in time, and I remembered the good times with my dad. His medical practice often took him away from home, but when he was home no one made me feel special and loved like he did.

Then there were those happy days playing with my sister, Mary Ann. We made sand pies and cakes and castles in our backyard sandbox. We climbed trees and swung about on our jungle gym. We did gymnastics on the grass, and when my dad was home he would clap and cheer for me and my sister. We sometimes played hide-and-seek or red rover with neighborhood kids. In those days, playing with Mary Ann and my dad, it seemed that I didn't have a care in the world. I always felt happy and accepted with her and my father.

With my mother, however, it was a different story. This is where my memories began to darken. Mom and Mary Ann did not get along well at all. Mom was an authoritarian, and Mary

Ann was a free spirit who defied Mom at every turn. Their frequent verbal clashes often escalated into angry screaming and ended in severe punishment for Mary Ann. The bulk of their arguments centered on how she fixed her hair or wore her clothes. I remember one incident in particular when Mary Ann rolled up her skirt at the waist to make it shorter.

Mom saw what she had done and sounded off, "No daughter of mine is going to school dressed like that."

"I don't see anything wrong with the way I'm dressed," Mary Ann retorted.

"That skirt is way too short. You go take it off right now and put on one that's decent."

"No! I like this one and I'm going to wear it."

"Don't you talk back to me, young lady! You're not going to wear that skirt, even if I have to rip it off of you."

After a few more verbal exchanges, Mary Ann relented and changed skirts. But as we walked to school, she rolled it up to make it even shorter than the one she changed out of at home.

It wasn't just clothes that set off explosives between Mom and Mary Ann. Anything could do it. I remember when Dad had a new house built for us, Mary Ann did not want to leave her neighborhood friends. To thwart the move, she often removed the "For Sale" sign from the front yard. Mom always put it back and punished Mary Ann severely for her defiance.

After Dad and Mom divorced, Mom moved us to Phoenix. When we reached high-school age, Mary Ann often sneaked out at night, sometimes returning in the early hours of the morning. She seldom got caught, but when she did, the screaming confrontations between her and Mom were like two cats howling in an alley.

I hated those confrontations and the punishment Mom so often inflicted on my sister. I didn't want any part of that, so I developed a quiet personality, speaking rarely as I watched and observed other people. I was always the good girl, obedient and compliant. On the rare occasions when I did something wrong, Mom never failed to let me know, not only lashing out in anger but also expressing deep disappointment in me. I hated that. I hated it even worse than the anger. Her angry threats frightened me, but my deepest fear was not that she would harm me physically; it was the feeling of being such a disappointment to her. I felt that I was letting her down, and I did all I could to prevent incidents that would arouse her anger or her disapproval. I worked hard at pleasing her. Unlike Mary Ann, being a good girl was important to me.

In my effort to avoid conflict, I seldom asked my mother for anything, unless it was something I really needed. One morning as I was getting dressed for school, I began to feel weak and unsteady on my feet. It happened to me now and then. As I think back on it now, it was probably due to low blood sugar. I sat down, told Mom how I felt, and asked her to please bring me a piece of toast. She refused and called me a hypochondriac. Her refusal to help even in that simple way angered me, but I did not show it. I think Mary Ann either helped me to the kitchen or brought me something to eat.

When I was fourteen, a girlfriend at school invited me to attend a Young Life club at someone's house. I kept going, and at a summer camp I came to know Christ. I was excited about my conversion and couldn't wait to tell my family about it. But none of them had any interest, and I could tell that Mom was a bit hostile to the idea. It showed particularly when I got up on Sunday morning and left everyone to go to church. My relationship with Christ was a double-edged experience for me. While my faith in him made me feel loved and safe, my family's lack of interest made me feel sad and somewhat isolated.

I saw nothing unusual or abnormal about any of my family's dysfunction. I was coping quite well with my environment, and I went on my merry way thinking I was living a normal childhood. I had no basis of comparison to make me think otherwise.

After my two panic attacks, one challenge to the illusion that I had experienced a normal childhood was the dreams I began to have at night. I related these dreams to Linda when I could remember them, and she was convinced that they had meaning. Though she never claimed to have a supernatural gift of interpretation like that of Joseph, who explained the dreams of Pharaoh, she seemed to have a knack for finding meaning in these dreams.

In one of the early dreams, I found myself outside somewhere, surrounded by several young children, all hungry and clamoring for me to give them food. I tried to feed them, but they turned down everything I offered. Then another woman came into the dream bringing sandwiches and baskets of Kentucky Fried Chicken. The children immediately left me to flock around this new benefactor and ravenously consume all the food she gave them. I just stood there feeling confused, useless, and like a complete failure.

When I related the dream to Linda, she became my Joseph—or perhaps more appropriately, my "Josephine"—and explained to me what the dream could mean. The children represented the little girl I was discovering inside me. Though I had become highly proficient at taking care of others, I did not know how to take care of her. When the children in my dream turned to another person for help, it symbolized the childlike Barbara inside turning away from me to find someone who could meet her needs better than I could. This naturally made me feel inadequate. Linda encouraged me to assure the childlike Barbara that the adult Barbara was capable of taking care of her and that I would not neglect her as her mother did. But it would not be a quick fix.

I remained diligent in my journaling, taking care to record all the memories my childlike Barbara revealed, all I could pull up on my own, and my reaction to what was going on around me in the present. The little girl did reveal a few scenes from my past and enabled me to discover some areas of dysfunction I had glossed over as an adult. But she revealed nothing helpful in my search for the debilitating trauma that was causing my present anxiety. Clearly, she was holding something back—something painful and emotionally troubling. I began to feel discouraged, thinking the whole thing had become an exercise in futility.

Linda was not discouraged, however, because she saw progress. So I kept on keeping on, hoping against hope that a breakthrough would come in God's good time.

Little did I know the horrific shape that breakthrough would take.

4

The Big Breakthrough

I can't remember ever laughing so much. Seven months had passed since my aisle 9 panic attack, and it was Steve's birthday. We were gathered in the private room at the Bamboo Club in Scottsdale to celebrate. Almost forty friends and family members flanked Steve and me, sitting at two long tables facing one another. Servers scurried between the tables, while family and friends talked, laughed, and enjoyed one another and the mouth-watering Pacific Rim fare. Everyone was having a blast, taking turns toasting—or more often roasting—the birthday boy.

At the conclusion of the meal, we have a tradition of honoring the birthday boy (or girl) with what we call "The Affirmation Exercise." Family and friends are encouraged to think of one positive character trait they see in the one being celebrated and share it with everyone. It usually starts with these words: "I remember this one time when Steve and I were ..." Most of the guests shared funny or heartwarming stories about Steve's generosity, his love of travel, and his appetite for adventure.

I laughed along with everyone else, but the merriment I exhibited that night was a far cry from what I was feeling inside. I was in considerable physical pain. I had been experiencing abdominal cramps and intestinal pain long before the party. But I didn't want to ruin the birthday plans, so I said nothing to Steve about it. Besides, after dealing with the panic attacks and their aftershocks, I didn't want to burden him with yet another of my ailments to deal with. I wanted him to bask in the accolades of family and friends. But the more he basked, the more my abdomen throbbed. I was more than ready for the festive celebration to end.

Finally, it did end. I was delighted that the evening had gone so well, but honestly, at that point, the only thing on my mind was getting home and resting. I was tired—really tired, and it was a deep tiredness seeming to emanate from the marrow of my bones. It was even more debilitating than the chronic fatigue syndrome I had dealt with since my panic attack seven months before. The pain increased by the hour.

I went to bed immediately after arriving home from the party, but the pain became so intense that I couldn't find a position that brought relief. Sleep was out of the question. By 2 a.m. Steve was driving me to the ER. They began running tests, and it wasn't long before the problem was revealed. My intestine was 97 percent blocked by a tumor. They gave me two choices: either have the tumor removed or I would die.

By noon that day I was in surgery, where the doctors removed eighteen inches of my colon and constructed a colostomy. To make matters worse, the tumor was cancerous. Just when it finally looked as if life might get back to normal, I was about to start a six-month program of chemotherapy while dragging a colostomy bag at my side and sporting a chemo port in my chest.

With the double whammy of anxiety attacks and cancer, the life I now faced was about as far as we could get from what Steve and I had planned after selling the business. I will spare you a running account of the grim details of coping with chemotherapy, but anyone who has experienced the ordeal will tell you that it's hardly short of hell on earth. Some who have been through it say that if their cancer recurs, they will simply put their lives in God's hands rather than plod through that dark valley again.

For the next several weeks, I existed in a continuous cycle of pain, nausea, sleeplessness, debilitating fatigue, weekly trips to the clinic, and countless medications. Add to this the fact that I was dealing with a colostomy bag and still trying to dig out that stubbornly stuck emotional pain from my past, and you can understand why I was a basket case.

To borrow from Ecclesiastes, that period of my life was not "a time to laugh." But as I soon learned, it was "a time to heal." It was Linda who pointed this out to me. Needless to say, throughout this ordeal I had good days and bad days. Actually, it would be more honest to say that I had bad days and really bad days.

I remember once when Linda came the day after I had completed a round of chemo and asked how I was feeling.

"Terrible," I moaned. "I feel like I've been flattened by a steam roller."

"Oh, good!" she responded with her typical upbeat brazenness. "That means you're vulnerable and we can work."

I probably glared at her as if she was Ivan the Terrible reincarnated, but what she said was true. When I was on my back and hurting, I was indeed more vulnerable. My defenses were down, which meant I was more open to uncovering the source of my PTSD simply because I lacked the strength and will to hold that door to my past closed.

As it turned out, during those bad days I made tremendous progress toward my emotional healing. So much progress that it soon became apparent that cancer, the "Big C," was, in fact, my friend. The debilitating chemo treatments created just the environment I needed to open myself up to the hidden secrets of my past that were imprisoning me.

The big breakthrough came shortly after I had arrived home from the hospital after receiving chemo through the surgically implanted port in my chest. I sat in the La-Z-Boy, my body exhausted, my stomach churning, and my mind foggy. Linda came and began her usual attempt to aid me in getting in touch with memories from my past. Seeing my defenseless condition as a golden opportunity, she sat down beside my La-Z-Boy.

"How is the childlike Barbara feeling today?"

"She feels about like I've been feeling," I said.

"So you have been in touch with your childlike self," Linda replied. "I'm glad to hear it. Why don't you tell me how she is feeling right now?"

"She feels frightened, sad, hurt, rejected, and alone."

"I am so sorry to hear it. Why does she feel that way? Did someone hurt her in some way? Did someone attack her or abuse her?"

"No, I don't think anything like that happened."

"But your childlike self is hidden down deep in the dark, isn't she? Why does she stay there?

"I think she's afraid, and she feels safe there."

"What is she afraid of?" she asked.

"I don't know. Maybe she's afraid of being left alone. Afraid of being abandoned or something."

"Why is she afraid of being abandoned?"

"I—I don't think I know. I haven't gotten that far with my childlike self. And I don't want to talk about it anymore, Linda."

"But we must talk about it, Barbara," she persisted. "We may be getting close to a breakthrough. Why is your childlike self afraid of being abandoned?"

"She's afraid of being alone."

"But she is alone now. You have her shut away where she can't be touched. And she will stay alone until you allow her to come out to be loved for who she is—for who you are. If she doesn't come out, those who love her cannot wrap their arms around her and make her feel safe."

Session after session with Linda brought me closer to the realization that what the childlike Barbara was feeling was exactly what I, the adult Barbara, was still feeling. Deep down I had a fear of being abandoned and left alone. In my head as an adult, I knew that at least Father God loved me and would always be there for me. But somehow, it seemed that the childlike Barbara didn't even trust Father God. And despite my head knowledge that God loves me, my feelings were not getting the message. My feelings for God were still tainted by mistrust that God would always be there for me—a distrust rooted in some yet-uncovered experience that had happened to me as a child.

I remember reading a scriptural account of some parents who brought their children to Jesus to be blessed. But his disciples told the parents not to bother him:

> When Jesus saw what was happening,
> he was angry with his disciples. "Let the
> children come to me. Don't stop them! For
> the Kingdom of God belongs to those who
> are like these children. I tell you the truth,
> anyone who doesn't receive the King-
> dom of God like a child will never enter
> it." Then he took the children in his arms
> and placed his hands on their heads and
> blessed them. (Mark 10:14–16)

My childlike Barbara needed to hear and believe that: Jesus wants you to come to him so he can take you in his arms. He is a safe place to share your hurts. You can trust him to love you regardless of whatever you tell him. You don't need to be afraid any longer. He loves you with a perfect love, and his love casts out all fear.

The adult Barbara needed to introduce the childlike Barbara to that kind of God—the real God who loves and accepts us without condition. I began to read the Psalms, trying to allow the words of Scripture to penetrate into the deepest parts of my being.

The LORD is faithful in all he says; he is
gracious in all he does. The LORD helps
the fallen and lifts up those bent beneath
their loads. All eyes look to you for help;
you give them their food as they need it.
When you open your hand, you satisfy the
hunger and thirst of every living thing. ...
The LORD is close to all those who call on
him, yes, to all who call on him sincerely.
(Psalm 145:13–16, 18 NLT*)

Even if my father and mother abandon
me, the LORD will hold me close. Teach
me how to live, O LORD. Lead me along the
right path. (Psalm 27:10–11)

What happened in the ensuing days attests to the truth
that the Word of God is indeed sharper than any two-edged
sword. Those passages began to cut through the darkness,
to unlock the door, to penetrate the barrier the childlike Barbara had erected against any attempt to reach her. Slowly I
began to remember. I began to see images emerging from
deep within my emotions and swirling about as if file drawers
in my mind had tipped open, allowing their contents to float
about in random chaos. One of those memories seemed to
rise up and loom ominously above the others.

"I ... I think ... I think I just remembered something," I said
to Linda during one of our sessions, my voice quaking as I felt
reluctant to say more.

"That's good, Barbara," Linda said gently. "Just try to
relax and tell me about it."

"I … I just remember the scene, but not what led up to it. I'm not even sure where we were, but I can see it all in my mind's eye. I was nine years old, sitting in the back seat of our car behind my mother, who was in the driver's seat. Someone else was in the back seat with me … I think it was Mary Ann, and maybe Rob. I knew something awful was happening, and I was beginning to whimper."

"That's good, Barbara," Linda encouraged. "Go on and tell me what you see."

"As … as I sat there in the car, my … my stomach seemed tied in knots, and I began crying in earnest. My dad stood outside the car. His hands were on the driver's door, and he was leaning forward, talking to my mom." I paused again. My voice could not get past the lump growing in my throat.

"Go on, Barbara," Linda urged gently. "You are doing just fine. This is exactly what you've needed to do for a long time. What did your father say to your mother?"

I swallowed hard and continued. "I don't remember Dad's words, but I knew he was telling Mom goodbye. I guess we kids had been told already, or I would not have felt so … so miserable. Then Dad finished talking to Mom and turned to look at me. 'Goodbye, honey,' he said as he raised his hand in a final farewell. 'Goodbye, and I am so sorry.'

"Then my mother drove away. I was now bawling as if my heart had been ripped down the middle. I turned to look at Dad through the rear window. He just stood there, forlorn, shoulders drooping, hands hanging at his sides, looking so utterly isolated and alone. I wanted desperately to go to him, to hug him, to stay with him. I could not stop crying."

My voice broke several times as I told the story. Finally, my emotions completely overwhelmed me, and I began to cry my heart out as if I were that little nine-year-old girl again. At that moment, I felt that I was that little girl. I felt again the deep pain and grief that had broken my heart when my father left. I loved my dad as if he were God, and he loved me—or so I had thought until that day. Distanced as I was from my mother, he was the most important person in my life, and I could not understand why he left me.

I emotionally concluded that my own dad didn't love me enough to want to be with me. I must have done something to make me unworthy of his love, or he would not have abandoned me. That wasn't true, of course, but that's what my young emotions had reasoned. Nothing had ever hurt me so much. I cried convulsively as Mom drove away, just as I was crying convulsively in my room in Phoenix as I told the long-suppressed story to Linda.

That memory was so terrible, so traumatizing to that poor little nine-year-old girl that she remained entombed in the darkness that descended like a shroud over her soul in that terrible moment, convinced that there must be something wrong with her. She was unlovable; otherwise, her father would not have abandoned her. That was reality as she perceived it. To hide the real Barbara, whom she was convinced nobody could love, she closed herself off from scrutiny and remained confined to the darkness. As I grew into adulthood, I left the real Barbara locked inside that darkness and began to wear my mask of people-pleasing activity to make myself appear to have value. After all, if my own father could not love the real me, how could I expect love from anyone else?

Linda suggested we take a break to give me time to regain my composure. But we both felt a sense of relief, even of elation. The dam had broken, and the long-pent-up hurts amassed behind it could now be released.

After giving me a drink of water and asking if I was okay, Linda continued: "How did your mother take your father's leaving?"

"She expressed anger, but never shed a tear, at least not in my presence. Nor would she tolerate my tears. We had not gone two blocks before she took care of my crying in short order. She whipped over to the curb, slammed on the brakes, turned to me, glowering, and said, 'You stop that crying this very instant, young lady. Your father is gone and that's the end of it. We're not ever going to talk about him again. Do you understand? Never again! Now you dry your eyes right now!'

"I did my best to stifle the sobs and bury my hurt. That's what our family did. My sister, my brother, and I were expected to stuff our feelings. We were never allowed to talk about why my dad left or how we felt about it. In fact, negative emotions were not allowed in our family at all. If you displayed anger or frustration with things not going your way, you were forced to go to your room until you got your emotions under control. Such feelings were off-limits."

"Did you manage to maintain a relationship of any kind with your dad?" Linda asked.

"Not much of one," I replied. "Every summer we three kids were allowed to spend a short time with him. I loved those times. They were like holidays. One thing I remember in particular was that at home Mom basically rationed our food. I don't mean she starved us or that we plodded around emaciated and hollow-eyed. But there were no elaborate meals, no second helpings, no snacks, and no snacking between meals. With Dad, however, meals were like feasting at a banquet. I could always eat as much as I wanted and feel free to ask for more.

"Once we returned home, we could not speak of him and heard nothing from him until the next year. We did receive birthday and Christmas gifts, but no letters. If we sent gifts to him, he returned them with this explanation: 'I can't accept any gifts from you because your mother probably paid for them.'"

"What did he mean by that?" Linda asked. "Was it some kind of deal he had made with your mother?"

"I never knew why he did that, but I do know that I felt it as rejection, and it hurt me deeply. Even my gifts were not good enough."

Linda could now see the pieces of my puzzle beginning to fit together. As she explained it to me, "Your father's leaving and his refusal of your gifts fueled your sense of abandonment until it festered into a deep sense of unworthiness that embedded itself deeply into your childhood psyche. Your mom forced you to stuff your emotions, which meant you were never able to process the hurt of your father's abandonment. Since that feeling was never dealt with, it remained swollen like an unhealed wound, festering over time until it finally burst and spattered its toxins within the grown-up Barbara."

Linda was leading me to see the reasons for my lack of self-esteem. As she pointed out, the causes of my feelings of inadequacy were twofold, rooted not only in my father's leaving but also in my fear of my mother. I could see that Linda was right. It explained why I wanted nothing to do with conflict.

I hated the fights between Mom and Mary Ann, but what really scared me were the threats Mom hurled at her.

I remember one recurrent threat in particular: "If you keep this up, young lady, I'm sending you off to the Kent House for Girls." When that threat didn't work, Mom would say, "I'm going to give you away to the next person who walks through that door."

These threats didn't frighten Mary Ann, but they scared me out of my wits. I thought my mother meant what she said, and I wondered if she would give me away too. My father's leaving made abandonment seem a very real threat, and the contentious atmosphere in our home reinforced that fear. To avoid being sent away, I had to appease my mother at all costs, and that meant I must refrain from expressing my true emotions. It took a lot of energy to keep my pain and feelings suppressed. But fear is a powerful force, and it succeeded in burying those defining traumas deeply enough not to interfere with my life, at least for many years.

One telling incident that showed how I coped occurred when I was in junior high school. The girls I hung out with at that time could sometimes be quite mean. Five or six of us were talking together outside the school building when Karen, a friend of mine, saw me and approached our group.

One of the girls pointed at Karen and sneered, "What kind of dress is that?"

"Yeah," another girl chimed in, "Where did you get it? At the Goodwill store?"

"No, she got it out of a Dumpster!" another girl added as the others laughed.

The girls kept it up, laughing and making fun of Karen. I wanted to defend my friend, but I was afraid they would attack me next. I stepped back to distance myself from the harassing girls, yet I said nothing. Though these girls were what I called my friends, I remember thinking I could not trust them. The safest course was to keep my feelings to myself and just be invisible.

Aside from my fear of confrontation, I also feared that my own clothes were not up to par. Mom was highly critical of how I dressed. She had pretty good taste in clothing, but she never taught us girls how to select colors, styles, or fabrics. I didn't trust my ability to choose clothing that pleased her, so I dressed quite conservatively and hated shopping, which made me very unlike all the other girls I knew.

By the time I reached high school, my emotions were solidly entombed. When Steve and I started dating, we spent a lot of time hanging out with friends. I could listen to their conversations, sense their varied emotions, and get a pretty good feel for who they were. But I couldn't express much of myself. I could talk well enough to keep conversation going, but I wasn't in touch with my feelings; they were buried too deeply to be reached. That made it difficult for others to get to know me. I hungered for the intimacy I was missing, but I had learned at a young age that sharing yourself with others was too big a risk for two reasons: first, it could bring up emotions and hurts better left safely buried, and second, if I revealed the real me, they probably would not like what they saw.

Linda used these revealing stories from my past to help me realize that all my people-pleasing efforts and all my busyness and doings were attempts to prove that I was acceptable and worth loving. I wanted people to care about me and to like being with me, but deep within I didn't feel worthy of it. This feeling had become embedded in that little nine-year-old girl so many years ago when her daddy abandoned her.

While unearthing these long-buried memories was painful—it was as if a time machine had transported me back to a war zone—it also gave me a sense of accomplishment, of relief, even of euphoria. I realized, however, that uncovering the trauma that had so affected my life was only the first step. I now knew the source and reason for much of what had shaped my subsequent life, but there was much work to be done before that pain was fully expressed and processed so that healing could follow. I still had a steep path ahead of me.

While I hated the cancer, and even more the long ordeal of chemo that followed it, I could not help but give thanks to God for the blessing it gave me in making me vulnerable enough to release my grip on my bottled-up past.

I wrote in my journal on October 30:

> God had to put me flat on my back to get my attention. He wants me to stop "doing"—running on the treadmill—and start "being." I am in the process of integrating my emotional self with my rational self. What an exciting journey!

In finally uncovering the pain of my past, I had penetrated a barrier and unlocked the door behind which I had been entombed. Now free of my long imprisonment, I could begin to find emotional healing. Little did I know that this metaphor of freedom from dark confinement was not as descriptive as I had hoped.

As I was about to discover, uncovering my past was very much like opening a can of worms.

5

Uncovering Additional Hidden Hurts

I had just returned home from physical therapy when I began to feel weak and woozy. I knew from experience what was happening: it was one of my low blood sugar attacks. While I understood what to do, I was alone at the time, as Steve was out and my usual caregiver had taken off early.

I made it to the kitchen, opened a can of orange juice, plopped into a soft chair, and began sipping. These attacks always left me weak and fatigued, and sometimes I slipped into a twilight state where I could not articulate my thoughts clearly. This was not happening at the time, yet I felt uneasy being alone. So I called Steve on his cell phone and told him what was going on. Though I didn't ask it, I hoped he would drop whatever he was doing and come home to be with me.

"Well ..." he responded, "I'm over at Jim's house, and we're right in the middle of putting siding on his daughter's playhouse. Are you in trouble? Do you need me to come home?"

I could tell by his voice that he didn't want to leave. So I said, "Oh no, don't worry about it. There's no crisis, and I'm feeling better now. Go ahead and finish your project."

I was not feeling better, but my old unconscious learned behavior of people-pleasing took over and I told the little white lie because I didn't want to inconvenience Steve. But rather than leave my feelings hanging in limbo, I followed Linda's directive and recorded my reaction in my journal. Here is that entry as I wrote it, first in my normal handwriting and then adding my childhood Barbara's response with my left hand:

Adult Barbara

Yesterday when I got home from physical therapy I called Steve to tell him about my low blood sugar attack. I thought he might want to come home and be with me. He was busy helping a friend put siding on a playhouse.
I could tell he didn't want to leave—so I told him I was feeling better when I actually wasn't.
How are you feeling about all that?

Childlike Barbara

I feel sad, left behind, resentful, insecure, afraid, unimportant, useless, pitied, weary, wrung-out, tired, betrayed, lonely, cheated, helpless, confused, afraid, rejected, unwanted, frustrated.

This string of negative emotions expressed strong reactions I would never have acknowledged in my adult compliant mode. By releasing my childhood self to express feelings I had long been in the habit of repressing, I began to acknowledge my true emotions, allowing them to come to the surface to be recognized.

One thing I did not expect from the journaling process was how it opened up a whole new world, the existence of which I had never acknowledged. The process reminded me of those brightly painted wooden Russian dolls shaped like fat bowling pins. When you lift off the upper half of the doll, you find a slightly smaller doll inside it. That one also opens to reveal a third doll. The third one opens to reveal yet another, and the process of revealing additional dolls continues long after you think there cannot be another to be revealed.

Opening up my past and freeing that little girl inside me was like that. Her revelation of my defining childhood trauma was only the first step—the first memory to be revealed. As I made daily entries in my journal, it became clear that I had layers and layers of suppressed hurts and memories to be healed.

The next one that revealed itself, as the incident with my low blood sugar indicates, was that my relationship with

Steve was not everything I had made it out to be in my mind. Beneath the placid surface of our marriage churned some hurts and feelings I had apparently glossed over and suppressed through the years. It seemed that after discovering my talent for repression as a little girl, I had in the subsequent years developed that ability into a highly sophisticated art.

As a young bride, I dreamed of sharing my life with Steve and enjoying the happiness of being with the man I loved. But I had no real understanding of what induced love to deepen intimacy, especially when we hit a few rough patches.

At the beginning of our marriage, the euphoria of romantic love seemed to override the emotional baggage of my suppressed childhood pain, at least through the honeymoon. And for me, the honeymoon ended sooner than I had hoped. What happened? Simply put, life happened. As in every marriage, we experienced a conflict here, a trouble spot there, and a crisis of sorts now and then.

Two months after we were married, Steve set out to start a business. I was working as a teller at Valley National Bank, and my job kept a roof over our heads and food on the table. Steve spent long days trying to make the business go and often dragged home late for supper. On one of these evenings early on, I remember sitting in our living room reading a book when I heard the door open.

"I'm home," Steve called, punctuating his announcement by letting the door slam behind him. "What's for dinner?"

"It's in the refrigerator," I replied.

As he came into the living room, I didn't drop my book or jump up and rush to throw my arms around him and plant a lingering kiss of welcome on his lips, as you might expect a young newlywed to do. I didn't even bother to look up from my book. After all, it was long past 9 p.m. "I made a chicken dinner," I said. "I waited till seven and then just ate alone—like I did last night and the night before."

"Oh, that's okay," Steve said, waving it off as inconsequential. "I had chicken for a late lunch, so I'll just get some cold cereal. You wanna come in the kitchen while I eat? I can tell you how my day went."

Reluctantly, I got up and made my way to the kitchen to hear my husband crow over his day's accomplishments like a rooster who thought he had made the sun come up.

"Steve," I finally broke in, "I know you are working hard, and I understand that it's sometimes necessary to work late. But it would really help if you would just call when you're going to be late like this."

"Oh, of course. What was I thinking? I'm sorry. The day just got away from me. Sure, I'll call next time. But man, are things beginning to take shape. Wait till you hear what else happened today."

I wish I could say this sort of thing occurred rarely, but that was not the case. It became our routine. I came home from work, ate alone, and then sat down to read a book. Steve came home, usually after dark, all excited about his work and wanting me to get excited with him. It wasn't that I didn't care about the business he was trying to build—of course I did. But I was just hoping he would focus a little bit on building a marriage relationship with me. It seemed that his world revolved around his work. I appreciated that he wanted to be a good provider, but I just wanted him to be a good partner. He wanted to give me things, while I just wanted him.

I voiced my concern a little about Steve's workaholic tendencies, but not enough to raise any hackles or create tension between us. I avoided real conflict at all costs. So instead of opening up and letting Steve know how I really felt, I clammed up. Instead of blowing up, I gave up. Instead of holding on to the dream of a deepening relationship, I let go of it and accepted what I had. That is what the Barbara I had become always did.

Linda kept telling me that if a marriage relationship is to grow, it requires opening up and letting your spouse know what touches you deeply, what moves you, what challenges you, and even what hurts you. But I could not do it. Revealing your innermost feelings when you're most vulnerable isn't always easy, and for me, stuck as I was, it seemed impossible. Linda persisted, however, painting a beautiful picture of what can happen when your spouse is truly a safe place and you invite him in, and no one else, to experience your deepest passions and even your deepest wounds. That something special is intimacy. But for me, intimacy didn't come easily. My lifetime habit of repression stood in the way.

Instead of embarking on a journey toward intimacy, Steve and I settled into a marital existence in which we were together but not really connected. We were with each other, yet we both felt emotionally alone. Rather than growing a deepening love life, we accepted a surface relationship. The true dynamics of love were missing. We had not captured love's essence, its mystery—we failed to make love a journey toward intimacy that brought fulfillment and completion to each of us.

Typical of me, I didn't even realize our marriage was missing anything. With my numbed and repressed feelings, I didn't expect any better. This is just the way life is, I thought, so I accepted it as normal and drifted with the current, oblivious to the joy I was missing.

One of the things that attracted me to Steve was his love of life. He was always on the go, always excited about what he was doing, and always so full of energy. You could sense he was a man going somewhere, and wherever that was, I wanted to go with him.

Because Steve's life was fast-paced, mine became fast-paced as well. It had to be if I wanted to be with him. Consistent with the habits I had developed in childhood, I always went with the flow, and Steve's stream flowed like whitewater rapids. Just as I, as a child, had become the good girl who did what she was told and avoided conflict, as an adult I became the good wife who acquiesced to her husband and submerged her own feelings and emotional needs. I became a quiet but busy doer and careful peacekeeper.

You know already about the baggage from the past that I brought into the marriage. You will find as you read Steve's story that he also brought in a truckload of issues from his past. We never opened all those tightly sealed bags; we just set them in the dark, remote recesses of our minds where they could be ignored. At some point you'd think a couple would slow down long enough to address the standard "stuff" that comes up in a relationship. But with Steve on the go and me being so compliant, we just turned a blind eye to what we didn't want to see and kept racing on with life.

In the due course of time, we had two wonderful daughters who were the delights of our life. Raising the girls occupied my time and attention and kept me from addressing the intimacy issues between Steve and me. We loved each other to the extent that we understood love. But that was a real problem for us, as our emotional baggage from childhood hindered us from experiencing true relational intimacy.

6

Steve's Misconceptions of Love

Wow! That girl is a real looker!

That thought shot through my head the moment I saw the lovely, brown-eyed brunette pulling her math textbook out of her locker. It was the first day of school, and I was an eighth grader at Kachina Grade School. The math book was a good omen, for math was my next class. I watched as the girl tucked the book under her arm and walked down the hallway. I didn't know her name, but I wanted her to know who Steve Uhlmann was.

People who know me now find it hard to believe that I was (and deep inside, still am) an introvert. Introducing myself to a girl never came easy for me. But luckily, she turned into the doorway of my math class and took a seat three chairs from the back.

Yes! What luck! I thought.

Kids were streaming into the room, but the chair next to hers was still empty. I rushed to it and sat down, trying to think of something cool to say. I guess I thought *Hi, my name is Steve* seemed too plain and simple. And lines such as "Hey baby, what's your sign?" had not yet come into vogue. While I was groping for a scintillating introduction, the class started.

When the bell finally rang, I gathered up my stuff and heard something clatter to the floor beside me. The beautiful girl had dropped her pen. She didn't seem to notice, so I quickly scooped it up and gallantly presented it to her like a knight offering homage to a princess. "I believe you dropped your pen," I said, deepening my voice and using my best diction.

"Oh, so I did. Thank you so much." Her smile was like a pulsar dazzling the nighttime sky.

Perhaps that was not a very profound way to begin a lifetime relationship, but great oaks spring from tiny acorns. I walked her back to our lockers, and our trek from locker to math class and back to locker became our daily routine.

The more I was with Barbara, the more I liked her. Our romance continued throughout high school. The physical attraction was immediate. I enjoyed being with her not only because she was beautiful, but also because she was a great listener. With my introverted tendencies, that was the kind of companion I needed—one who seemed to approve and endorse my ideas and ambitions. We quickly became a pair— proverbial junior-high and high-school sweethearts who met as young teens and never again parted. She seemed enamored with my ideas and vision for our life together. She interjected few ideas of her own, but was a great champion for what I wanted to do in life and appeared excited about our future. That, along with her beauty, was enough for me.

As I'm sure you can see already, the relationship started off somewhat one-sided, and it pretty much stayed that way. But we both were oblivious to that imbalance and to the difficulties it would inflict on our future.

We graduated from high school and got married after my two years of college. I loved Barbara in the only two ways I knew how to love. The first way was doing things for her. I thought I was pretty good at doing loving things. Over time, especially when we got our financial feet on the ground, I provided for Barbara everything I thought a wife could want to make her happy—a nice home, fine clothes, a luxury car, elaborate vacations, etc.

The second way I loved her was through sex. The sex was great for me, and Barbara was always cooperative. Yet despite all this "love" I gave her, there was no deep emotional connection between us. But there was no great tension either. Even though I had a misconception about the nature of love, from my point of view the marriage moved along on an even keel and without any serious problems. Something may have been lacking, but I was totally oblivious to it.

Had you seen Barbara and me together during this period of our lives, you would have thought we were a close and happy couple. When we went out with friends, we laughed, had a good time, and enjoyed each other. Yet we didn't experience a relational intimacy that bonded us together emotionally. As Barbara has said in her story, neither of us sensed emotional fulfillment and completion in our relationship. We were together in many ways, but relationally and emotionally each of us was alone.

My college major was engineering, and to put myself through school I got a job as a part-time apprentice mold maker at a plastic injection molding company. After a few years, I decided to launch our own plastics molding company with a partner, Jim Price.

Developing this business pretty much took over my life. Looking back, it's hard to say whether I plunged my whole being into my business because I felt emotionally unfulfilled in my marriage, or whether I felt emotionally unfulfilled in my marriage because I put all my emotional energy into the business. At the time, of course, I was not aware that anything was lacking in our marriage. I thought things were rocking along pretty well. Little did I know!

What I most enjoyed about those days was the challenge of solving problems and meeting customer expectations. For me, good relationships were about delivering a quality product to a satisfied customer. I wanted to be known as a premier problem solver who could deliver. And that's precisely what our company became known for. We developed an industry-wide reputation for problem solving. We were able to design, develop, and produce plastic parts with a high quality that met demands as diverse as ink cartridges for Hewlett-Packard to precision medical components for Abbott, Lilly, and many other medical manufacturers. I'm convinced that this was why we grew so fast. And the larger we grew, the more I pushed to become even larger.

Barbara told of the early days of our marriage when I consistently came home from work after dark, of the isolation and aloneness she felt. But as oblivious as I was to her needs and focused solely on my own, I felt none of that disconnection. I thought she would be as excited about growing the business as I was. After all, I was doing it for us, wasn't I? That's what I told myself, but it was far from the truth. Looking back, I can see that my work essentially became my lover. It was there that I sought to find my value and worth as a person. Striving to succeed became my passion—the mistress I consorted with day and night. The more I possessed her, the more I became obsessed with her. With every achievement, the hunger to achieve more grew within me. I was forever on the run to accomplish greater things. But at that time, I had no idea that I was running in the wrong direction, chasing the wrong carrot.

In his book *Blue Like Jazz*, Donald Miller tells a story about Don the Rabbit who saw Sexy Carrot and decided he had to have her. He began to chase her, but she was very fast. He chased and chased and chased until finally with one last burst of strength, Don Rabbit lunged and caught Sexy Carrot. "The moral of the story," Miller wrote, "is that if you work hard, stay focused, and never give up, you will eventually get what you want in life. Unfortunately, shortly after this story was told, Don Rabbit choked on the carrot and died. So the second moral of the story is this: Sometimes the things we want most in life are the things that kill us."[7]

I knew that work wasn't a bad thing and that succeeding at what I did wasn't wrong. But it seemed I was choking on a pursuit of success that could never bring me the deep love and intimate connection with another person—a connection I needed and wanted. Work was my mistress, but it lacked the human element. So feeling relationally empty, I sought a human connection outside of marriage.

The business was growing to the point that we were establishing new plants in various other cities and countries. This demanded more and more of my attention and required considerable travel away from home. About nine years into our marriage, a business acquaintance introduced me to an escort service where I became involved with some call girls. Though I never consciously reasoned why I took this step, I think somewhere in my subconscious darkness I selfishly felt that I just needed a little more than Barbara could provide. And as long as she didn't know about my infidelity, no harm would be done.

I eventually owned up to my unfaithfulness to Barbara. Yet even in my confession, I maintained a defensive and self-justifying attitude: "I'm sorry I did it, and I'm sorry I hurt you. But I would never have wandered sexually if I felt I was getting the kind of loving I need at home." I even had the audacity to suggest that she read up on what a woman should do to make her man happy.

Although my unfaithfulness devastated Barbara and shattered her trust in me, her deep fear of abandonment and unworthiness kicked in to make her quick to forgive me. We sought some help through professional counseling, but her wounds remained unhealed.

I promised I would never consort with call girls again. We tried to put the incident in the past and move on with life. Yet my attitude toward sex remained unchanged. That is, I still saw the sexual connection between a man and a woman primarily as an act of pleasure meant to achieve physical satisfaction. I saw it as a need that my partner was supposed to supply for me. I had no clue as to the spiritual and emotional connection that God designed to accompany the physical act. At the time, I did not realize that sex was meant to be an act of giving rather than receiving, an act involving the whole person, including mind, emotions, and soul, and not just the physical apparatus.

Obviously, I was still clueless as to how to develop an intimate relationship with Barbara. Therefore, our marriage went on autopilot, cruising along in the thin atmosphere of emotional starvation that left both of us unfulfilled.

I kept my promise never again to consort with call girls. But with my skewed and self-focused view of sex, I suppose it was inevitable that I would still feel a desire to seek additional sexual pleasure to compensate for what I convinced myself I was lacking at home. So, having so nobly renounced the use of call girls, I allowed myself to indulge in pornography. It was easy to justify. Viewing pornography was not really unfaithfulness to Barbara. It involved no interaction with a real person. I figured since I wasn't involving anyone else or hurting anyone, what could be wrong with it?

I regret to say that at this stage of my life, I was not any better as a father than I was as a husband. I remember one telling incident when my daughter Pam was about seven years old. It was an hour after dark when I pulled into the driveway, arriving home from work. I got out of the car, fished in my pocket for the house keys, and realized I had forgotten them.

I rang the doorbell. Little Pam cracked the door open, leaving the sliding safety latch in place, and said, "Who is it?"

I jokingly said, "Hi there. Is your mommy home?"

"Just a moment. I'll go check," Pam replied in a monotone. She closed the door in my face and went to find her mom.

I was stunned. My own daughter, who should have recognized my voice instantly, thought I was a complete stranger. And why wouldn't she? I spent long hours at work and traveled often for our growing company. When I was home, I often left for work in the morning before my two daughters, Pam and Tracy, were even up. And I generally arrived home in the evenings after they had gone to bed. They hardly knew me. Back then I guess you would have been justified in calling me an absentee husband and father.

It wasn't that I didn't love Barbara and my daughters, and it wasn't that I didn't want to spend time with them. I just didn't know what love really was, which meant I didn't know how to make an emotional connection with my family. I connected better outside my home with my work than inside my home with my family.

Our marriage rocked along, and I suppose we coped well enough, mostly because neither of us realized what a real marriage could be like. With our truncated understanding, we didn't know we were missing anything. Our girls grew up, went off to college, and got married. The business flourished beyond all my early dreams, becoming a multi-national corporation with nine thousand employees working in plants around the globe.

When I got an offer to buy the business at a handsome profit, I decided to take the deal and retire early. I made grandiose plans for Barbara and me. We both enjoyed traveling, and I had dreams of exploring the parts of America and the world that we had not seen. I was really gung-ho about our plans and looked forward to our globe-trotting adventures.

Then suddenly Barbara's panic attacks and PTSD hit us broadside, blowing my travel plans out of the water. There is no question about it; Barbara's sudden health breakdown did get my attention. But I must admit that the timing of it left me pretty frustrated. How long would our travel plans have to remain on hold? No one seemed to know. And to be honest, I questioned whether her anxiety attacks were a real physical problem or just something going on in Barbara's head. As usual, I saw everything in simple, mechanistic terms. We needed to do what I did in my business: find the cause of the problem, fix it quickly, and move on. But because I couldn't fix this problem, I didn't know how to cope with the frustration. I felt that life had pulled the rug out from under me.

I followed all the doctor's orders. I hired caregivers to be sure Barbara would never be left alone. I brought in Linda, the perky life coach you have already met, to work with her daily to bring about emotional and spiritual healing. And I was attentive to her—more attentive than I had been in years. I wanted my wife to get well.

We needed to get on with our life.

7

Fear and the Lack of Trust

Steve's business was taking off, and keeping it growing and thriving demanded more and more of his attention. While his duties included much more travel away from home, his promise to stop seeing call girls seemed sincere. He repeatedly assured me he would never enter that world again. But a few years later he confessed to me that he had become a regular viewer of pornography. I did not discover his porn use, nor was he forced to confess. But he confessed freely because he wanted to be open and up-front in letting me know what he had been doing and that he was making excellent progress in overcoming his porn habit.

I did my best to accept his confession and apology at face value. I guess I should have felt honored that he was open with me in sharing his secret and making his confession voluntarily. Yet the fact that he had substituted pornography for prostitutes didn't help my feelings of inadequacy. It merely fueled my sense that I was not enough for him—that I could not satisfy his needs or measure up to the call girls and porn stars with their perfect bodies and sexual proficiency. My sense of worth plummeted to even lower depths.

Then came the empty nest. Several years later, Steve decided to retire early and sell the business, which had flourished mightily into an international corporation. While I remained home most of the time, I made it a point to stay busy. I filled my life with what a good girl and good wife should fill it with—good works. I became involved in several ministries. I joined the boards of foundations. I got involved with charities. I participated in women's groups and church events.

Then my aisle 9 crisis sent me reeling, and everything ground to a halt. My chronic fatigue syndrome followed by cancer and the ordeal of chemotherapy essentially put my life on hold.

I must admit that when all my emotional and physical crises came crashing down on me, Steve could not have responded any better. He seemed to drop everything to be with me. But I found myself conflicted even by his solicitous concern and attention. I knew that my health collapse had interrupted his plans for us to travel the world, and I couldn't help but wonder if he was really just trying to get me well quickly so we could get on with his agenda. I was afraid that if I didn't heal fast enough, he might give up on me. It was unfair of me to think this of him, but my old hurts and fears continued to steer many of my emotions. Here's what I wrote in my journal on September 20:

Steve is anxious for me to feel better and get back to my "old self." I'm afraid I don't want to go back where I was before. I was so easy to get along with, but it was not healthy emotionally.

Clearly, my need to share my real feelings with Steve was emerging from its long confinement, but my fear of sharing them still held me back. In addition to my fear, sheer habit and routine also added to my reluctance to risk tampering with the dynamics of our relationship. Over the years I had allowed Steve to make virtually all the family decisions, even when I would've liked to have a say in them. He would just let me know what he had decided about things and what my role in them should be. That always seemed to work because compliant little me went along with everything.

I remember one incident when we were just about to come home from a vacation. I started crying, realizing that I had spent our entire time just going along with whatever Steve wanted to do and had done none of the things I had hoped to enjoy myself. We walked along the beach every day, but I would have preferred sitting in a lounge chair just watching the waves for a while. Of course, it was my responsibility to tell Steve what I wanted to do. But my compliance with his strong tendency to lead was an example of my reluctance to voice my preferences, fearing that my ideas were not valuable enough to express.

Yet Linda continued to encourage me to speak up and set boundaries with Steve. The new, more mature Barbara— the one who was slowly getting in touch with her emotions—

was just beginning to understand a little of who she was and that she had individual opinions and desires. It wasn't that she necessarily wanted to oppose Steve; it was simply that she needed to gain a voice of her own.

To be honest, I was terrified at the idea of letting Steve know I might like to voice my opinion on what went on in our lives. So Linda took it upon herself to approach Steve on my behalf. That was a mistake!

I don't remember what exactly she said to him, but obviously it made him feel threatened or that his authority was being questioned. At any rate, he reacted with extreme negativity and expressed that reaction in no uncertain terms. Linda came back to me, almost in a state of shock, and said, "No wonder you're afraid."

In September Steve asked me to be involved with him on a project. Instead of telling him the truth—that I wasn't up to it—I just took the easy route and said okay. Then it hit me: I'm reluctant to say no to Steve out of an obsessive fear of abandonment. How silly of me! He's not going to leave me just because I say no to him! It was as if a light suddenly turned on. I was acting on an irrational fear of a nonexistent problem in the present that was rooted in a very real and rational fear lodged within me from my past. A fear that the childlike Barbara needed to face.

Journal: September 20

I couldn't say no to Steve because I still have a childhood fear of abandonment. I need to face that head on and allow my adult self to tell my little girl that she

is safe now. Steve is not going to leave me
no matter what happens.
This was a turning point for me. I can now
recognize when my irrational fears—that
were very real and rational as a child—
are interfering with my relationship with
Steve!

That was a defining moment for me. I consciously recognized the difference between my reality-based fears from
the past and my irrational fears in the present. In putting aside
those fears and pushing my true self to establish a voice in the
things that concerned my life, I was becoming a real person—a
mature person who could feel and respond emotionally. I was
gaining my voice, and God was giving me the courage to speak
up. And speak up I did. I wrote a letter to Steve:

Journal: October 30

Dear Steve,
We are on a rocky journey together—you
and me. The Lord has slowed me down by
physically allowing me to suffer a lot of
different things.
I think he is getting my attention to
change some things in my life. I was
pretty unaware of my feelings for so long
that I had forgotten what it was like
to feel. A lot of the feelings that are
bottled up are from childhood.

They have kept me from developing close connections with people, including you. We are closer now, as I have been working on telling you how I feel and how you can help me—explaining what I need from you.

I know this has been a hard time for you and you want to get me "fixed," so you are looking for ways to get me well sooner. I appreciate that, but I have been told this will take some time. I hope you can be patient with the process.

God is in control, and he knows what I am going through. He knows what kind of care I need. When I am doing better I will support you in your own healing journey. I love you!

Love, Barbara

My letter caused Steve to ask himself a few probing questions. One of the many fine things about Steve is that he does not allow his ego to stand in the way of honest intro-spection and self-appraisal. Was it possible that he had been too controlling, too assertive toward me? Could his past atti-tudes and behavior have contributed to my emotional strug-gles—or worse, perhaps even led to the collapse of my health? He began to face these questions honestly and directly, and as you will soon see, his self-assessment led him toward a new direction for his own life.

In 1963 when engineers began construction on the "Gateway to the West," the magnificent, 630-foot towering arch in St. Louis, Missouri, workers started building the two bases of the arch simultaneously but separately. Each side had separate crews, separate supervisors, separate sets of blueprints, and separate machines. Over the months, the two sides gained height, sometimes one side growing faster than the other. As they grew, each began to curve delicately toward the other until finally in 1965, they met perfectly at the apex of the arch.

Both Steve and I had begun to build a new life of authentic love and intimacy. Our procedure was much like that of the St. Louis arch builders. Though each of us worked separately, Steve on his life and I on mine, in one sense we were both working on the same construction. We both were rebuilding our marriage. Yet in another sense, his construction and mine were completely separate. Each of us had to reconstruct our lives around a new principle before we could meet at the apex of our newly formed arch of love.

That principle was authentic love, and the source of authentic love is God himself. If I was to love Steve with authentic love, I needed to follow Jesus' definition and example of love. He said I was to love God with all my heart, soul, and mind, and then to "love your neighbor as yourself" (Matthew 22:39).

The term neighbor in the New Testament doesn't mean the person next door. It literally means "near one"—any person within your environment who has a need for your love and care. Steve was my closest neighbor, and I needed to love him as I loved myself. But as you know by now, self-love was a big problem for me. How could I love myself when I felt essentially unlovable? Yes, I knew that God loved me, but I didn't feel I was worthy enough to receive his love. And if I didn't feel worthy enough to accept God's love, I surely couldn't feel worthy enough to love myself.

That was my dilemma—an inability to express authentic love because I couldn't love Steve as I loved myself.

8

Because He Loves Me, I Can Love Me

By now I was really into journaling, writing my thoughts and feelings both from the past and present, practically every day. It gave me an opportunity to reflect, express myself to God, and eventually express myself more fully to Steve.

At the same time, Linda was helping me realize that all my people-pleasing efforts and all my busyness were attempts to prove that I was acceptable and worth loving. I wanted people, especially Steve, to care about being with the real me, but deep within I still didn't feel that the real me was worthy of such care. This feeling was embedded in that little girl so many years ago when her daddy abandoned her. If the most important person in her world at the time didn't think she had sufficient value to merit his staying in her life, how could she expect anyone else to see her any differently?

I now realized how deeply that rejection hurt me. It essentially shaped my outlook and personality from that day forward. My father's abandonment, coupled with my sense that my mother found me unacceptable, fueled my sense of unworthiness, making it the defining essence of the grown-up Barbara. I was stuck in my childhood past, still feeling that my father's abandonment meant that I was essentially unlovable.

Again, like the cavalry in a Western movie, Linda galloped to the rescue. "Do your feelings always reflect reality?" she asked.

"Well, in a way, I'd say yes," I said. "Our feelings come as reactions to what happens to us, and what happens to us is our reality."

"Not always," Linda replied. "Sometimes your feelings arise from what you perceive as reality, while the true reality is something altogether different. For example, someone told me about a small boy who always ran and hid in terror of the postman when he delivered the mail. Why? Because the postman wore a pith helmet, and the boy had seen a movie showing soldiers wearing helmets killing each other in battles. He was afraid the postman might kill him. His feelings about the postman had no basis in reality."

"But the boy's feelings were real to him," I said.

"Yes. But that doesn't mean they reflected reality. Look at it this way, Barbara. Do you ever feel that God is distant from you? That he doesn't really love you as much as he loves some other people?"

"Yes, I do feel that way. Often."

"But in the Bible, God tells us many times and in many ways how dearly he loves us. That is reality."

Linda shared that God loves me with an everlasting love, that I am his child, that I am forgiven, that I am his master-piece, that I am redeemed, that I am not condemned, that I am chosen by God, that I am his friend, that I am hidden with Christ, and that I am his very own possession.* When she fin-ished, she looked at me and said, "You do believe the Bible, don't you?"

"Of course I do!" I replied, perhaps a little indignantly.

"Then you must believe God when he says you are dearly loved and cherished, which is what the Bible tells us."

"Well, yes, I do believe that God cherishes me dearly," I agreed, "but to be honest, it's hard for me to feel his love down deep most of the time. And when I don't feel it, it doesn't seem real to me."

"Let me ask you this," she said. "Do you feel he loves you more when you are doing things like serving on mission boards, coordinating benevolence, or teaching a women's class? And do you feel he loves you less when you are sick or fearful or angry or hurt?"

"Yes, I suppose I do feel that way."

"Yet you just affirmed that you believe the Bible when it tells you he loves you unconditionally. As you can see, Bar-bara, your feelings do not match up with the reality you know to be true. You know that God loves you unconditionally, yet you feel that he won't love you unless you perform—that he loves you for what you do rather than for who you are. Your

---

* Jeremiah 31:3; John 1:12; Colossians 1:14; Ephesians 2:10; 1:7; Romans 8:1; Colossians 3:12; John 15:15; Colossians 3:3; 1 Peter 2:10.

feelings and true reality are at odds with each other. The bottom line is always this: You are deeply loved even when you don't feel that love."

I nodded. I could see her point.

"It's important to realize that even if your emotions mislead you, they do reflect your real and valid feelings," she continued. "They are valid in the sense that they affect you with the full force of seeming real. But understand this: Your feelings about God's love do not align with truth. The truth is that you are worthy of unconditional love regardless of what your emotions feel. Does that make sense?"

I nodded again.

"The more you come to know God and how dearly he does love you, the more you will feel his love."

All that made sense. As I was growing up, the focus was on my doing rather than my being—what I did rather than who I was. Everything seemed to revolve around how well I performed in school and at home, how I looked, or how well I behaved. This feeling carried over into my adult life. For example, when Steve and I were going together, he often told me I looked beautiful. Of course, it made me feel good when he complimented me on my looks. But that feeling was tainted with another feeling: when he spoke of my beauty, I felt that he was actually saying I was sexually attractive. It made me feel that he loved me for what I had rather than for who I was.

I know that Steve did not mean to imply that my worth was based on my outward appearance. But I was conditioned to take such a compliment in that way. That was because from childhood I found my sense of value and worth was in what I did and how I looked.

The underlying problem was now perfectly clear: because of the perceived rejections I suffered in my childhood, I did not feel worthy of love. Therefore, I felt that I had to earn love by performing, by doing, by making myself valued by what I offered in the way of good works and acquiescence to the wants of others. I had no sense of innate self-worth. Or, to put it starkly, I did not love myself. How could I expect others to love me if I could not love myself?

The idea of loving oneself sets off alarms in the minds of many Christians. But shortly after Linda's lesson on the reality of God's love, I continued to study and learned that self-love is actually a biblical concept. We are leery of self-love because it seems dangerously close to selfishness, self-centeredness, and narcissism. We think immediately of the "Me Generation"—those younger people who seem to be so utterly self-absorbed and all about themselves, like the glamorous model in TV commercials who treats herself to the luxurious product "because I deserve it."

It's true that we are warned against making life all about self and focusing exclusively on our own interests and wants. The apostle Paul wrote, "Don't be selfish; don't try to impress others. Be humble, thinking of others as better than yourselves. Don't look out only for your own interests, but take an interest in others, too" (Philippians 2:3–4).

Paul's words give us a valid caution about the dangers of self-love. But I was learning that there is an enormous difference between the self-centeredness and narcissism that focuses on my own desires, comfort, pleasure, and needs, and the kind of self-love that recognizes my intrinsic value as God's own beloved creation. Linda was helping me realize that when Jesus said to "love your neighbor as yourself," he was strongly implying that I should love myself. And so I should. I have immense intrinsic value and worth as a human being simply because I was created by the hand of God in his own image. As someone has rightly said, "God doesn't make junk."

That fact gives me enormous value that needs to be provided for and protected. It gives me an obligation to respect and value myself as a person lovingly designed and created as God's masterpiece. This recognition is by no means an indication of self-centeredness. Caring for myself as God's creation is a godly thing to do. I was beginning to realize that if I don't value and love myself as I should, I wouldn't have the proper basis for loving Steve—my closest neighbor. That is why I needed to love myself unselfishly.

Steve was learning those same truths about the need for healthy self-love. As he put it, "Jesus was speaking from that premise when he said, 'Do to others whatever you would like them to do to you'" (Matthew 7:12). Everyone wants to be respected, treated fairly, honored, and recognized for his or her uniqueness. No one wants to be lied to, disrespected, cheated, or discriminated against. Such negative treatment violates our personal sense of self-worth. That internal sense of self-worth is what signals us to treat others as having the same value that we perceive in ourselves. So loving yourself properly is far from being selfish. In fact, some say that a proper understanding of our worth and value as God's creation helps keep us humble and guards against selfishness."

Steve reminded me that Paul wrote that a person is "not to think more highly of himself than he ought to think; but to think so as to have sound judgment" (Romans 12:3 NASB).

Paul wasn't saying we shouldn't think highly of ourselves; we simply aren't to think we are something more than what we really are. When we love ourselves as God intends, our love can serve the interests of others as we make their welfare and happiness as important as our own.

As biblical as self-love is, and as much as I wanted to love myself unselfishly, I still faced a few hang-ups that prevented me from feeling the unconditional fullness of God's love. I knew he loved me, but I could not shake the feeling that his full acceptance of me depended on my attitude and actions. Yes, in my head I knew better. I knew that this was only another of my erroneous feelings that had no basis in reality. But that feeling was there; it was real to me, and I had to deal with it.

Because of this feeling, the childlike Barbara especially had trouble believing—or more accurately, feeling—that she could safely open up the innermost thoughts of her heart to God. Surely he would disapprove of much of what she harbored there. Any emotional honesty before him would provoke the same kind of disappointment her mother expressed when little Barbara failed her. At least, that is the fear childlike Barbara felt.

I took the issue directly to God in a prayer. Here is what I recorded in my journal on April 10:

Lord, please help me. I'm not sure what to do. I need your wisdom, your guidance, your mercy and peace. I think my little girl is afraid of being punished if she expresses anger. I need you to help me feel safe and that I will not be punished for saying how I feel. I need to learn to trust you with everything.

I am frightened about the future, but I know in my head you are sovereign and you are there for me. I need you to move my head knowledge to my heart. Teach me, Lord, how to do that. Help me to come to you when I am weary, tired, scared, angry, resentful, disappointed—you want to hear it all.

I feel inadequate, which is okay because you are my strength. When I am weak, then I am strong.

I feel weary, but you told us to come to you when we are weary and tired and you will give us rest. We are to take your yoke upon us because you are gentle and humble at heart and we would find rest for our souls. So I am choosing to put on the yoke of suffering with you and learn from you.

Slowly but surely, the profound truth that God loved and accepted me without condition was sinking in. As my suffering intensified, I hung onto that truth with all my might.

The pain from my continuing ordeal was unrelenting. The panic attacks, chronic fatigue syndrome, and then the cancer followed by chemotherapy took a heavy toll on my body, and

I began to wonder how much longer I could endure it. There is something about unrelenting pain that not only wears you down physically, but also flattens you emotionally. As you can probably sense, it challenged me spiritually as well.

Yet through all this suffering—the physical pain, ongoing nausea, weakness, discomfort, sleepless nights, and even the mental and emotional turmoil—I came to experience God in two altogether new ways. I began to see a different God than I had known before.

First, he was becoming more real to me because I identified with his suffering. Through my own suffering, I began to identify with the God-man, Jesus, knowing that he fully understood what suffering is like. While on earth he experienced ridicule, rejection, abandonment, misunderstanding, and betrayal, not to mention the bloody scourging by the Romans and his six hours of unspeakable agony on the cross. This Scripture resonated with me as I read it:

> Since he himself has gone through suffering and testing, he is able to help us when we are being tested. ... [He] understands our weaknesses, for he faced all of the same testings we do, yet he did not sin. So let us come boldly to the throne of our gracious God. There we will receive mercy, and we will find grace to help us when we need it. (Hebrews 2:18; 4:15–16)

Second, I began to understand the character of God, or, you might say, even his personality. I began to feel a definite attachment to him. Ever since Linda had revealed him to me as a loving Father and a safe place, he began to assure the childlike Barbara that she had permission to unload her heart and soul and spill out to him her deepest feelings. He wanted to hear what she felt and what she experienced. He wanted her to know that he loves her, that he hurts for her and wants to bring healing to her wounded heart. As I slowly learned to trust his assurance, I dared to reveal my raw and pent-up emotions to this God who is caring and kind, and who said, "I will never fail you. I will never abandon you" (Hebrews 13:5).

This was exactly the kind of God I needed. A God who wants to be my Father—who wants me as his cherished daughter. A God who wants to hear my deepest sorrows, to feel with me my deepest pain. A God who wants me to be open to him. He was becoming my special refuge and my safe place to be real as I suffered and gave him all my struggles.

Journal: June 25

Lord, I give you my anxiety, my hurt, my insecurity, my frustration, my confusion, my fear, my weariness, my feeling of being forgotten. You have told us to cast all our anxieties and cares on you, for you care for us. If I am to continue to suffer, Lord, it is to get a taste of your suffering. I am trusting you to give me the strength and perseverance to get through each day, each week, each month. I want to glorify you even through this time.

During those long, painful days and sleepless nights, I wrote the following four verses in my journal and read them often. They took on fresh new meaning to me.

Be merciful to me, Lord, for I am in distress; my eyes grow weak with sorrow, my soul and my body with grief. My life is consumed by anguish and my years by groaning; my strength fails because of my affliction, and my bones grow weak. (Psalm 31:9–10 NIV)

But as for me, I watch in hope for the Lord. I wait for God my Savior; my God will hear me. (Micah 7:7 NIV)

My flesh and my heart may fail, but God is the strength of my heart and my portion forever. (Psalm 73:26 NIV)

I will be glad and rejoice in your unfailing love, for you have seen my troubles, and you care about the anguish of my soul. (Psalm 31:7)

When I read Bible verses like these prior to my struggles, I believed them and accepted them rationally, but I did not feel them. They did not reach into my emotions and touch the deepest part of me—the wounded childlike Barbara. But in time, through Linda's counseling, my journaling, and God's help, I experienced the full force of God's unconditional love for the childlike Barbara who was locked away from all relationships, feeling afraid, unimportant, abandoned, unwanted, and paralyzed with insecurity.

For so long I ignored the childlike Barbara—this pent-up apparition whom I called my former childhood self. I knew how to take care of everyone else, but I didn't know how to take care of her. She was there wanting to be noticed all along. Jesus wanted to let that girl with such childhood hurt know that he loves her, yet she remained in the darkness, locked away by fear.

Because those deep childhood hurts weren't healed, they found a way to get my attention through the panic attacks. I'm so glad they did. Through God's love and the help of Linda, this childlike part of me finally felt safe enough to emerge from her long and lonely imprisonment in darkness and step confidently into the light. I felt Linda and God embracing the childlike Barbara. I, too, eventually wrapped my arms around that little girl and loved her with all my heart. And by God's grace we started to merge as one.

To remind readers of what I said earlier, there was never any confusion in my mind, in Linda's mind, or in Steve's mind that the "childlike Barbara" I've referred to throughout this narrative was actually a separate person from myself. This was by no means a psychological multiple personality case. Yet since my childhood, I had not been an integrated person. I was a living contradiction. Part of me was stuck in the past, huddled in fear and tightly clutching a misconception about who I really was. The other part of me lived in the present, wearing a mask to prevent anyone from knowing what I thought to be true—that I had no intrinsic value worth loving.

But when the adult Barbara uncovered the childlike Barbara, the two Barbaras moved toward each other. The childlike Barbara began to release her fear and move toward maturity, while the adult Barbara began to discard her mask and move toward a healthy, biblical childlike attitude of openness, love, freedom, and trust. Or, to put it another way, the childlike Barbara and the adult Barbara began to merge into a single integrated being. As they became more integrated, that unified being began to experience wholeness. I was becoming real, like the Velveteen Rabbit. I was becoming the real me God intended me to be from the beginning.

Linda helped me to coax the little Barbara out, and I embraced her, wept with her, and brought comfort that had been so long coming. Over time, and it still continues, I have come to know the real me—a person who has a heart to please others, who loves God, and who is gentle and kind and desperately wants to be involved in people's lives. I am learning to be open and honest, faithful and loyal, and willing to give of myself to others. I have become someone I can love.

The next step for me was to find a path that would lead me to an intimate relationship with my husband. That meant I must introduce Steve to the real me. For that to happen, I had to be vulnerable and open up to him. If he was to be allowed in, I had to trust him with my feelings.

I could see that Steve was changing too. He had become more attentive, and he was beginning to listen without judging when I expressed what I felt. That was a good start, but for Steve to be invited in fully, I needed to trust him fully. He needed to be a safe place. And given what I experienced in the past with him, thinking of him as a safe place was a big problem.

I had already been hurt in my marriage, and that hurt came from the man who said he loved me, yet betrayed me. Steve had confessed his infidelity to me years before, and even though I did my best to forgive him, I had a hard time trusting him. But by the grace of God, Steve had embarked on his own journey of discovering the pain of his own past, finding healing, and coming to grips with how to live out an authentic love. He and I both realized we were called to love in a very special way—called to love like Jesus!

9

Love Her Like Who?

I was raised in a nominally Christian home and became a nominally Christian young man in my teenage years. But I did not allow my Christianity to get a solid grip on my life or interfere seriously with my wants. Throughout the early years of my business, I went through stretches when I did not attend church at all. Well, maybe on Christmas and Easter—that is, if I wasn't traveling at the time.

But on a beautiful March day, Barbara and I attended a Josh McDowell conference in Phoenix. There, I rededicated myself to the Lord. I began to study the Bible seriously and make a serious attempt to follow Christ. But my efforts were often fumbling and imperfect. I still had a long way to go before I could keep the old Steve down long enough for God's Holy Spirit to assume the driver's seat. Barbara's crisis did a lot to help me do that.

After taking what I considered proper steps to deal with Barbara's anxiety attacks, three incidents conspired to get my attention and set me back on my heels. The first of these involved my pastor. A short while after Barbara's second attack, I sat in his office, lined wall-to-wall with shelves sagging with books, as all pastor's offices are. This was an alien environment for me since I'm not much of a reader. In fact, someone once joked that I have written more books than I have read. (That is, I think it was a joke.) But there I was, looking across the desk at my good friend, Pastor Darryl.

"What's on your mind, Steve?" he asked.

"Well, to tell the truth, I'm frustrated," I replied. He knew of Barbara's difficulties, of course, so I plunged directly into my complaint: "Barbara's breakdown happened at a most inconvenient time for us. We had just reached the stage of life where we were free to travel as we had always wanted to do, and then, boom! This problem explodes in our path and we've got to put everything on hold. It's really frustrating."

"You're frustrated because your wife is ill?"

"It's not just that," I said. "You've got to understand, Darryl, that this stuff is mostly in her head. Sure, there's a medical issue involved, or she wouldn't be dealing with chronic fatigue. An endocrinologist is prescribing medication for that, however, and it will soon be taken care of. But this other thing, this anxiety issue, is a problem that's all in her head."

Pastor Darryl just sat there patiently, letting me vent my frustration. Finally, he spoke. "So what is it that you're troubled about? What's your question?"

"I guess more than anything, I want to know how I'm supposed to respond to Barbara's issues—especially when

I'm not convinced they are real. I want to be a good Christian husband and respond with Christlikeness, but what does that look like? What am I supposed to do?"

"Steve, there is only one answer to that. Focus on one thing and only one thing." Pastor Darryl paused for the longest time, just looking at me.

"Okay, I'm listening," I said, looking squarely at him. "What is that one thing?"

He smiled and in a gentle voice said, "You are called to love Barbara like Jesus loves you. Focus on that one thing— your calling to love your wife as Jesus loves."

I thought about that many times after meeting with Pastor Darryl. What a simplistic answer! Love her like Jesus loves me. What on earth does that mean? Of course, all of us are called to love others as Jesus loves us. But how was that applicable to my particular situation?

I had a wife who was being plagued with panic attacks for God-only-knows-why. What was I supposed to do? How was I to respond to all that? Businessman that I was, I wanted a step-by-step plan, some specific course of action that could help me get through the situation. A call to "love like Jesus" seemed simplistic, elementary, and without tangible meaning.

The second incident involved Linda Milner, Barbara's life coach. I won't recount the incident, but apparently I unloaded my anger on Linda with both barrels. I honestly don't remember losing my temper with Linda, but I don't doubt that it happened. I know I was capable of it. I remember a previous incident that occurred at the office. We had just ordered a new state-of-the-art injection molding machine. This would be the largest of all of our machines, and acquiring it involved a real financial stretch for us. We needed to get this massive piece of equipment into production, making money to pay for itself as soon as possible.

The machine was more than two weeks overdue, and the broker was not returning my calls. He finally called when we were in the middle of a staff meeting. I took the call and learned that the broker had chosen to ship the machine via an independent trucker. This monster weighed ninety thousand pounds, which is over the limit for US interstate highways. Rather than disassembling the machine, separating the injection end from the clamp end, and shipping it on two trucks, he had chosen to use the independent trucker who would travel on back roads to avoid the weigh stations.

During the course of this conversation, I became more and more enraged, screaming invectives at the broker in ever-escalating volume until finally I slammed the phone down. When I finished my tirade and turned around, the staff was gaping at me wide-eyed, like a deer caught in the glare of the headlights.

Though I don't remember the incident, apparently I gave Linda a dose of the same bitter medicine I had unloaded on that foolhardy broker. After I was reminded of this encounter, I began to wonder, *Is it possible that I am being too controlling with Barbara?* I didn't believe it, but the question was raised and it wouldn't go away.

The third incident that got my attention was a letter that Barbara wrote to me after she had begun to journal and uncover her past traumas and feelings. She had been getting closer to God and was allowing him more control over her life. She was beginning to overcome some of her fears, which enabled her to express her true feelings instead of hiding them to gain acceptance. She revealed that she knew I was impatient to have her "fixed" so we could get on with my plans, and she begged me to have patience with her as she struggled through the healing process. Finally, she gently hinted that I might find a few issues rooted in my own past that needed a bit of healing.

My first response to that letter was not positive for two reasons. First, I was not interested in dredging up issues from the past. The past was past, and nothing about it could be changed. I was a forward-looking guy, and I saw no advantage in looking back.

My second concern about the letter involved the future. It was apparent that the Barbara I had known since the eighth grade was changing. I had loved her compliance, her willingness to follow my lead in the dance of life. But this "new Barbara" wanted to be more open about her own wants and needs. Would I be able to cope with this new Barbara? Would I know how to love her as she emerged from the cocoon that had so long confined her, and spread her wings, becoming less compliant, more open, and maybe even assertive?

When I added these three incidents together—Pastor Darryl's "one thing"; Linda telling me that Barbara was afraid of me, or at least afraid of letting me know of her wants and needs; and finally Barbara's letter with its subtle revelations—I began to wonder if perhaps I should take a serious look at myself. Maybe a man is like a company and needs to take a regular inventory. All three incidents seemed to suggest that some of the marriage disconnect between Barbara and me could be as much my doing as it was the result of her repressed past.

I began to ask myself questions. Was it possible that I had been too controlling? Could my attitudes and behavior have contributed to her emotional struggles? Did I need to look into my own past to find the source of my attitudes and tendencies?

Linda was keeping me up to speed on Barbara's progress—and Barbara was definitely making real progress. She was getting to the root of her problem and making visible headway in coming out of it. Seeing the process work so well with Barbara induced me to question whether my "leave it in the past" approach was working for me. I began to think about some of my childhood pain, and as those memories made me wince, I thought to myself, *Perhaps I do need some healing after all.*

So I began to explore some of my own painful childhood memories.

***

"What are you doing, young man?" Mom barked as she stuck her head into my bedroom.

"Nothing really," I replied. "Just reading a book."

"Well, put it down and get cleaned up. We're leaving in a few minutes, and you look awful. When we get back, I want you to clean up this nasty room." As Mom walked away, I heard her mumble under her breath, "Pig!"

Growing up, I don't remember ever receiving any positive affirmation from my mother. It seemed that she continually complained about what I didn't do right, which was just about everything. I never remember getting a hug from her or hearing her say, "I love you." I never felt that I was important to her. In fact, I was convinced that she saw me as a nuisance and would have been happier if I had never been born.

Mom was an alcoholic. I don't know what happened in her past that made her so unpleasant, but unpleasant she was! In fact, she was simply mean. No one who came in contact with her ever disputed that fact.

One day in particular is vividly burned into my memory. My dad, who did love me and showed it, wanted to bring a little fun into my life. In late spring, he purchased a plastic swimming pool and set it up in the backyard. He had inflated the pool and was now in his swim trunks as he filled it with water. "Go get your swim trunks on, son," he called to me, grinning from ear to ear. "We're about to have a good time."

I was so excited! I got my swimsuit on in minutes and dashed out into the yard again, ready to make a big splash.

Suddenly Mom's voice pierced the air. "Ernest Uhlmann, what in the world do you think you're doing?"

"Steve and I are about to have a little swim party," Dad replied.

"Oh no, you're not!" she retorted as she bolted off the porch yelling obscenities. "It's too cold for swimming."

Before I knew it, my mom was literally jumping on my dad as he attempted to defend himself. He would never hit her, and before the attack was over, she had inflicted several bleeding wounds on his back. After she stalked away, I remember applying mercurochrome and bandages to several bleeding scratches on my dad's back. Mom's verbal and physical abuse of Dad was common in our home, yet it always disturbed me deeply.

Eventually Dad had enough of Mom's atrocious behavior and divorced her. I envied him more than blamed him. He got away from an abusive wife. But I was stuck with an abusive mother.

My dad was something of a hero to me. Everyone respected him, except of course my mother. He was a real estate investor and a hotel developer. He owned two hotels and was proud of his success. He was also a Scoutmaster, and I remember with fondness all the camping and hunting we did together and sometimes with my uncles.

Dad took a real interest in me. He could tell how down I felt when Mom berated me and beat on him. I'm sure that he thought if I could accomplish things like he did, I might feel better about myself. So he put me to work. Unlike other fathers, he didn't give me an allowance. He thought money would mean more to me if I worked for it, and that working to earn what I had would give me a sense of self-worth. I worked around the house mowing the lawn, weeding the flower beds, and doing other chores. When I got older, I worked during the summers painting at the two hotels Dad owned. He never hesitated to tell me how proud he was of the work I did.

Work became my escape. I could never do enough to please my mom. I never felt a connection with her, but I did feel a connection to the work I did with Dad. His consistent praise of my work and accomplishments always made me feel good. But as he attempted to teach me the value of a dollar and of hard work, I inadvertently began to attach my worth to my accomplishments. I didn't realize it at the time, but now

I'm sure that somewhere deep within me I believed that Dad was prouder of my accomplishments than of me. Or perhaps that he was proud of me because of my accomplishments, and not merely because I was his son. As a result, I became a performance-driven man, an overachiever who set high goals and tried to prove my worth by working hard to accomplish more than anyone around me.

So it was natural for me to show my love by what I could do and provide for a person. In my mind, love was performance-based. And prior to all the health issues that came crashing down on her, it was the same for Barbara. She too had been brought up to base her value on her performance. But she was now on a journey out of that trap. She was learning how to get in touch with the truth about her authentic self—how to become "real" by opening up to allow another to know her and love her.

Barbara had been updating me on how she was opening up to God and expressing to him what she felt and what she feared. She said she was learning to know God as a loving and safe person. She was no longer trying to hide from him the truth about who she really is—a healthy blend of the childlike Barbara and the adult Barbara. As a result, she claimed she was gaining a deeper, more intimate relationship with God.

I got the hint. She was hoping I would become a safe person to open up to as well. I think she was hoping I could experience the same kind of love she was experiencing. I could see that this new path Barbara was on was leading her to a good place. Her struggle to be real was producing highly positive results, and I began to hunger for the same thing. I, too, wanted to be real so I could experience an authentic love with Barbara. How could I go about finding that kind of love? Where should I begin?

As I asked these questions, Pastor Darryl's words kept ringing in my head: "You are called to love Barbara like Jesus loves you. Focus on that one thing—your calling to love your wife as Jesus loves you." Well, to my analytical mind, that challenge made the next step obvious. So I set out on a quest to discover what that kind of love is like. I started at the only place I knew to start—to study what it means to love like Jesus.

10

The Meaning of the Ring

In my pursuit to love my wife as Jesus loves me, I asked this question: How serious is Jesus about me loving Barbara as he loves me? I found two Scripture passages that answered that question clearly. Jesus said:

> A new commandment I give to you, that you love one another: just as I have loved you, you also are to love one another. By this all people will know that you are my disciples *if* you have love for one another. (John 13:34–35 ESV)

> This is *my commandment,* that you love one another as I have loved you. … These things I *command* you, so that you will love one another. (John 15:12, 17 ESV)

Okay, Jesus is so serious about how I am to love that he made it a command. The next step was to explore the nitty-gritty of what it means to love as Jesus loves. I delved deeply into the Scriptures and made a thorough study to discover exactly what Christlike love means.

The first thing I learned is that Christlike love has a consistent object. Jesus' love is always other-focused. The people he loved in the Bible always took precedence over himself. The cross is the supreme example of other-focused love—the willingness to endure unconditional self-sacrifice for the well-being of the other.

Second, I learned that Christlike love is always a serving love. It looks for the needs in the other person and addresses those needs by supplying what is lacking, giving what is required, and doing what is needed. Christ's willingness to perform the lowly task of a servant and wash the road-dusty feet of his disciples is the supreme example of his serving love. He consistently met people at the point of their needs.

Finally, I learned something about the character of Christlike love. As Paul tells us, it is always patient, kind, and gentle, and does not boast or make a big deal about what it does for the other person. The more I learned about Christ's love, the more I struggled to know just how that kind of love was to play out in my day-to-day relationship with my wife. I think I had the concept of loving unselfishly pretty well embedded in my head, but I still needed to transfer that knowledge from my head to my heart. I didn't want to love solely because I was commanded to do it; I wanted to be motivated to love with my whole being—mind, will, and emotions. I wanted to be irresistibly drawn, without any external compulsion, to throw my entire being into other-focused love.

Sometimes radical changes to our lives occur in the strangest of ways, often through incidents or events that alter our outlook and attitudes when we least expect it. That was the case with me. One unexpected incident transferred my desire to love Barbara unselfishly from a mere intellectual wish to a heartfelt reality.

Soon after Barbara's first panic attack in the grocery store, some unusual bleeding sent her to her gynecologist. This was before we discovered her cancer. The gynecologist diagnosed the problem as a benign fibroid tumor and scheduled a routine dilation and curettage (D&C) procedure to remove it.

When they moved her from the operating room to her bed, I was allowed to see her, and I was shocked at what I saw. She was still unconscious from the anesthesia, and her skin was as gray as putty. She made no movement at all. At first, I didn't even think she was breathing. She looked dead. I was scared half to death. At that moment I realized with my whole being that *I did not want to lose Barbara.*

As I stood there, it seemed that for the first time I saw beyond the immediate physical condition of my wife. I saw a woman who had been hurting emotionally for many years, and I felt welling up from deep inside me an overpowering, empathetic sense of the hurt she had endured. I began to feel stabs of her pain, her anguish, and her sense of aloneness. You might say it's natural to feel sympathetic toward a spouse who is hurting. But this was much more than just natural sympathy. I had never before felt this deeply moved by compassion toward Barbara for the agony she had been going through.

When she came out from under the anesthesia, those emotions rose up and overwhelmed me. I began sobbing and telling her how much I hurt that she hurt. I repeated over and over that I loved her. That wasn't like me back then. There was nothing forced about any of this. I simply could not help myself.

For the first time in my married life, I was truly focused on Barbara. Whatever she needed was what I wanted to give. What was important to her was becoming important to me. I began to be sensitive to what she cared about so I could care about it too. These were my first steps toward loving Barbara like Jesus loved her. The scales were falling off my eyes, and I began to see the real Barbara and truly love what I saw.

This was a new beginning for me. It signaled an important transition in my life. I don't want to overstate my growth in love and leave the impression that from that moment on I was the poster boy for Christlike love. I still had a considerable stretch of road to travel and much to learn. The panic attacks and the D&C merely opened me to the introductory lessons. When Barbara's cancer invaded our lives, it ushered me into an advanced class where I learned far deeper insights into loving with a Christlike love.

Barbara came home after her cancer surgery, weak and unable to do many things for herself. I made it a point to have a young woman at the house practically at all times, caring for her every need. Yet I tended to hover about her wherever she was in the house—in bed, on the couch, at the table, or in her recliner—trying desperately (and perhaps somewhat comically) to do my part. I wanted to be there for her. Our conversations often sounded something like this:

"Can I get you something to drink, dear?"

"No, thank you. I'm fine for now."

"How about a pillow to prop you up a bit higher?"

"No, I don't need to be propped up."

(A few minutes later...)

"What about a book to read. Can I get you a book?"

"No, thank you. I don't feel like reading right now."

"Do you feel a little cool? I can get you a blanket."

"No, I'm just fine, Steve. Please, I'm just fine. I just need to rest."

Barbara is not one to complain, so it was hard for me to know how I could help her. I'm afraid my attempts made me more a nuisance than a helper. I probably became like nurses at hospitals who wake up the patient to administer a sleeping pill.

Then an opportunity presented itself to me that changed everything.

With eighteen inches of Barbara's colon removed, she had to wear a colostomy bag to cleanse the toxic waste from her system. She could change the bag itself, but every two or three days a seal needed to be removed from her abdomen, cleaned, relined with a sealant, and the bag replaced and secured with a ring.

This was akin to changing a baby's diaper, an analogy that is fitting for two reasons. First, no one enjoys changing a diaper. It's a messy, distasteful task that offends both our fastidiousness and our nostrils. Second, people change diapers not because they enjoy the task or even because they feel forced to do it. They change diapers because they want to change them. Why do they want to change them? Because their deep love for the baby draws them to want only the best for her, and they know it's best for the baby to have her diaper changed. This motivation completely transforms the task of diaper changing, turning it from an unpleasant, distasteful duty to a joy for the good it does the baby.

That is how I approached changing Barbara's colostomy bag ring. I didn't recoil from the task. I didn't hate to do it. I wanted to do it and found joy in doing it because I love Barbara. The ring became a new symbol of the kind of love Jesus expressed. Tending to that ring week after week made Barbara realize that I truly wanted to make what was important to her important to me. For those weeks at least, the ring that secured the colostomy bag was more significant than the gold wedding ring I had placed on her finger so many years before.

Through these experiences, I was beginning to understand something about Jesus' kind of love. My love was supposed to be more than a set of things I did to fix situations or make things better. It was to be a deep and overriding concern for the welfare of my beloved. My new sense of care for Barbara began to change the way I saw her.

Love as it was expressed by the pre-crisis Steve followed a standard pattern: a dozen roses now and then, a box of chocolates, a dinner at a restaurant, or a night out on the town. But now it was dawning on me that real love is an unselfish mindset that in my pre-crisis existence had been utterly foreign to me. In other words, the idea of loving Barbara was beginning to move me from just doing things for her to becoming someone to her. Rather than getting caught up in doing and fixing things for her, I began to focus on being in love with her. That meant focusing more on her by discovering who she was becoming and what she needed from me relationally and emotionally.

I recognized the experience with the colostomy ring as a breakthrough for me. I had taken another step toward loving as Jesus loves. God is always delighted when we take our first steps in his direction, just as a human father delights in his child's first baby steps as she learns to walk. Yet while God is pleased with our baby steps, he is not content that we should always toddle like babies. Ultimately, he will be pleased with nothing short of the firm, purposeful strides of a mature Christian walking in the footprints of Jesus.

That's how it was with me at this point in my progress toward loving maturely. No sooner had I taken those first exhilarating steps than God pointed out to me that I had many more steps to go—more relational potholes in my path that needed to be patched to keep me from tripping.

Linda, Barbara's life coach, had been signaling to me that my emotional abandonment of Barbara, my past sexual infidelity, and my use of porn had inflicted pain that still lingered in Barbara's psyche. The simple apology I made years before was merely a crude patch job that had never been adequate to cover the breach I had torn in our relationship.

Linda's message resonated with me, because my new commitment to love as Jesus loves was bringing me face-to-face with how my actions and attitudes had contributed to Barbara's emotional pain. It's not easy to admit that you are a contributor to your wife's deep-seated hurts, but that was the journey God had set me on—a journey to discover how deeply I had hurt not only Barbara, but also myself and God.

I committed myself to yielding to God's incessant prodding, and that, as it turns out, became a defining moment in bringing healing and deepened intimacy into our relationship.

11

What's Love Got to Do with It?

"Oh, come on, honey. Let's go ahead and do it. After all, we love each other, right?"

"But Steve, we should wait until we're married."

"Why does that matter so much when we truly love each other? It's a way I can let you know I really love you. And it sure lets me know you love me."

"I know, but it just doesn't feel right. What would God think?"

"I'm sure he will understand. We're going to get married, so why should the technicality of a wedding ceremony make so much difference?"

My exploration of my past dredged up this exchange and several similar ones between Barbara and myself before we married. The pressure I put on her shows plainly that I didn't understand the biblical perspective on sex, which means I had an unhealthy attitude toward sexuality. My incessant sexual pressure on Barbara did nothing to establish trust in our relationship.

It didn't help that she wasn't taught a healthy perspective of sex either. All her mother ever told her was that she needed to protect herself from the sexual advances boys would inevitably thrust at her. Consequently, Barbara's primary emotional response to sex was one of guardedness and hesitation. But such passive defenses were no match for my misguided but incessant pressure tactics.

Stuffed into the emotional baggage we lugged into our marriage from childhood were our tangled ideas about sex. I tended to think that love was spelled S-E-X. The physical pleasure of sex was my primary focus, and it was essentially divorced from any emotional or relational connection to Barbara. In my mind, sex and love were on two separate tracks, and it never occurred to me that the two should ever meet or merge.

Tina Turner recorded a hit song back in 1984 titled "What's Love Got to Do with It?" The song portrays two people attempting to maintain a connected relationship based solely on the physical act of sex without allowing love to enter the equation. The lyrics tell us that an attraction that is all about self-gratification has nothing to do with love.

But that was pretty much my own approach to sex. I thought great sex was a primary indicator of a good relationship. And because sex was a big deal, I figured I was a good lover.

The truth is, however, that sex was not designed to be the foundation of a great relationship. Using sex for that purpose turns the truth completely on its head. Sex alone cannot create a selfless, loving relationship—but an intimate, loving relationship where both partners are devoted to pleasing each other can create fantastic sex. Unfortunately, I had no inkling of that perspective. Consequently, my misguided view and self-focused practice of sex contributed to our lack of intimate connection.

This misguided view of sex led me to commit my two most obvious offenses against Barbara in our marriage. My newfound desire to love as Jesus loves led me to readdress how severely those offenses had hurt Barbara. Years ago, I had apologized to her for my involvement with call girls, and she graciously forgave me. In fact, it seemed that she forgave me much too easily, and I was too calloused to see the reason. It was because my infidelity hit her in the place where she was most vulnerable—in her insecurity about relationships, her fear of being abandoned again by a man as she had been abandoned by her father. My infidelity opened that particular wound, and she forgave quickly for fear that a serious confrontation might drive me to leave her as well. Because of this deep wound in her past, my betrayal caused much deeper damage to her than I realized. A sacred trust had been broken, and a simple "I'm sorry and I won't do it again" was not sufficient to bring healing.

Obviously, it didn't help that I turned around and substituted porn for prostitutes. While I apologized for that indiscretion as well, I sensed Barbara didn't feel that I saw that much wrong with what I was doing. My attitude seemed to be that porn was just a way to release sexual energy without hurting anyone.

I could not have been more wrong. And I realize now that far too many hold the same misconceptions about porn that I held. Allow me to digress from my story for a moment to pass on a few things I've learned about pornography.

Sadly, research confirms that many people, both men and women, have the same cavalier attitude toward pornography that I had. A recent study finds that barely half of American adults say porn is wrong (54 percent). According to the research, a majority of people believe that overeating is worse than viewing pornography (58 percent).[8]

Many men and women, even Christian men and women, don't believe anyone is being hurt by their porn use. They see it as a victimless activity. Many others do believe porn is wrong, yet they are so drawn to the enticing images it offers that they engage in it anyway. Tragically, the sheer number of couples affected by pornography is staggering. There are a lot more people into porn than most of us realize.

When the Josh McDowell Ministry commissioned the Barna Group to research pornography use in America, Barna surveyed nearly three thousand US teens and adults, including ministers. The results, called "The Porn Phenomenon Study," shows that porn use has reached deeply into the church. The research indicates that 87 percent of Christian men between the ages of thirty-one and fifty periodically come across internet porn, and 63 percent actively seek it out.[9] This Christian porn use is not limited just to people sitting in the pews. The study found that 64 percent of youth pastors and 57 percent of senior pastors admitted to presently or previously struggling with the use of internet porn.[10]

I didn't correlate my porn viewing to any pain or damaging effects it might have inflicted on my wife. And because of that, it was easy for me to become a repeat offender. David Ferguson drives this truth home in his book *Never Alone* when he says, "Until we grasp more fully how we have hurt our spouses and the Lord, God's work of repentance in our lives will be hindered, and we are likely to keep on repeating the pain and hindering oneness."[11]

As I indicated above, even after I did sense that I had hurt Barbara, my apologies didn't do much to bring about healing or rebuild trust in the relationship. I understand now that the depth of my apology could not reach any deeper than my comprehension of the pain I had caused her. My apology conveyed a minimal understanding of her pain, and therefore it felt correspondingly minimal to her. It did little or nothing to address the emotional wound inflicted by my straying sexual attention.

As I began my attempts to love Barbara as Jesus loves her, I realized that I was called to keep my sexual relationship with her pure. I began to see how God's plan for intimacy called for an exclusive relationship that connected me with Barbara and Barbara with me. Because that relationship was by nature exclusive, the lustful desires and impure thoughts that led to sex outside marriage were violations of my sacred vows to love her only. That is why my porn use hurt Barbara. In fact, it was also hurting me and God. My self-centeredness and self-serving gratification hit the trifecta—I was hurting myself, my God, and my wife.

I Was Hurting Myself

The only way a person, especially a Christian, can believe that porn hurts no one is to close his eyes to the many articles, books, and blogs showing how many lives have been ruined and crimes committed as a result of pornography addiction. Logic alone should have told me something. Pornography deliberately promotes sexual arousal but provides no meaningful and lasting means of satisfaction. Porn viewers must somehow deal with that frustration, either by repression, masturbation, or sexual predation, none of which is a healthy response to sexual arousal.

For the Christian, which I was at least nominally at the time, there is even less excuse. As the apostle Paul wrote:

> You can't say that our bodies were made
> for sexual immorality. They were made for
> the Lord, and the Lord cares about our bod-
> ies. ... Run from sexual sin. No other sin so
> clearly affects the body as this one does.
> For sexual immorality is a sin against your
> own body. (1 Corinthians 6:13, 18)

I had ignored this clear warning against sexual temptation. But when I read it again after my commitment to start loving Barbara as Jesus loves her, it spoke to me in a fresh new way. One fact discovered by medical scientists helped me to understand this Scripture. Neurologists have found that the endocrine system of the human body manufactures a bonding hormone designed to promote feelings of intimacy with our sexual partners. It is called oxytocin. During sexual arousal, the brain releases this chemical, which prompts feelings of connectedness, affection, and attachment. Oxytocin works to reinforce the bonding of my wife and me—to reinforce and deepen our love relationship as a couple.

When I was sexually aroused by pornography, oxytocin was released, but its bonding activity was misdirected. Instead of feeling attached or bonded to a real person, I was becoming bonded to a set of images on a monitor. Neurologists say that the more a person interacts with porn, the more the released oxytocin programs the body to be stimulated by pictures rather than by a real person. This means my use of porn was doing more to me than merely releasing sexual energy; it was programming my body to respond to pixels on a screen and diminishing my response to my flesh-and-blood wife.

It bears repeating: There is a reason God tells us, "Run from sexual sin. No other sin so clearly affects the body as this one does" (1 Corinthians 6:18). As God convicted me of the problem created by my porn use, he did it, in part, for the benefit of my marriage. He wanted my sex life to help me feel more relationally connected to Barbara and more spiritually connected to him.

I Was Hurting God

In confessing to Barbara and repenting of my infidelity with call girls and pornography, I thought I had made things right with the only one I had offended. Of course, as a Christian I confessed and repented to God as well. I knew I needed his forgiveness and that these sins needed to be added to those Christ took to the cross. But I did not realize how a man's sexual unfaithfulness hurts God.

The account of an event in Israel's history woke me up to that fact. For readers who may not be familiar with much of the Old Testament, I'll summarize the story.

King David was on the flat roof of his palace one evening when he noticed a beautiful young woman bathing on a roof below. Her naked beauty aroused his lust, and he sent for her to be brought to his chambers. Shortly afterward she turned up pregnant. David knew it was his doing, because the woman's husband was away fighting in David's army. To cover his sin, David had her husband brought to the city on the pretense of giving a report. But when the loyal soldier would not go home to his wife, refusing to indulge in privileges denied to his fellow warriors back on the battlefield, he signed his death warrant. David instructed his general to place this soldier in a military position where he would certainly be killed, so that David could marry his widow and cover up his sexual sin.

After these terrible deeds were done, Nathan the prophet came to King David with a story of a selfish rich man who took a poor man's one and only pet lamb, killed it, and served it to his guests. David was outraged that the rich man would have the audacity to take from someone else when he already had so much. "The man who has done this will surely die!" he declared.

The prophet then put the unvarnished truth straight to the king: "You are that man!" (2 Samuel 12:7). David immediately understood his offense and said, "I have sinned against the Lord" (2 Samuel 12:13).

What stunned me about this story was that last sentence: "I have sinned against the Lord." I could see that David had sinned against his own wives, and I could see how he had sinned against the woman he seduced. And he had certainly sinned against her husband. But how had he sinned against the Lord? Yet after committing these terrible sins against all these people, David saw his primary offense as being against God. How so?

I found the answer in what God said to the king:

> I gave you your master's house and his wives and the kingdom of Israel and Judah. And if that had not been enough, I would have given you much, much more. Why, then, have you despised the word of the LORD and done this horrible deed? (2 Samuel 12:8–9)

Let's unpack that bit of Scripture. God had wrenched the kingdoms of Israel and Judah away from their first king because of his failures and had given the monarchy to David. David already had five wives, great riches, spectacular success in battles, and the favor of the people. In other words, God had given him everything a man could want and would have given him "much, much more." Yet despite all these abundant gifts God so lavishly poured on him, David reached out and took something that did not belong to him.

You know how it feels to buy the latest computer or smartphone that has multiple features right at your fingertips. For a while you think, *Man, this is the greatest thing I've ever owned. Look at all the stuff I can do on this gadget.*

Did it ever occur to you that you should think of your own body with the same sense of wonder and excitement you feel when you first begin to use one of these gadgets? Just look at this masterpiece of engineering God has given you! It has flexible extensions equipped with five-pronged tools that can be manipulated to perform all kinds of gripping, holding, twisting, and hurling tasks. Your body has two extensions providing unlimited mobility. It has appendages that pick up sounds and aromas. It has devices to enable vision, communication, reproduction, and taking on fuel and converting it to energy. In addition, its entire surface is equipped with sensitive sensory capacity, and the entire organism is controlled by an omnicomplex, multilevel computer. As if that was not enough, it is equipped with consciousness and an enormous capacity for pleasure, which it is capable of receiving from almost every appendage and organ that makes up its composition. And it's all yours, given to you freely by God to use for your good and his glory.

Not only has God given me this incredible masterpiece of a body, he has also given me another being with a body constructed much like my own but with complementary features that bring to my life immense joy and pleasure in more ways than I can count. This complementary being is the finest gift God ever gave to man. The one he gave to me is called Barbara, and she is a beautiful replica of the original model that God created for Adam.

I can imagine what God might have thought when he created Eve and first brought her to Adam: That man I created is really going to love this. I can hardly wait to see the expression on his face when he sees her. I can hardly wait to see the joy they share as they build their life together and realize how truly marvelous each is to the other.

I don't doubt that God thought something similar when he brought Barbara to me. So what did I do with this incredible gift?

I did essentially what King David did. Despite the fact that God had given me the most wonderful and delightful gift he had ever given a man, I said, "I think I'll try out a few call girls. I think I'll get a few sexual kicks by looking at flat, inanimate pictures of girls instead of focusing exclusively on Barbara's beauty."

I can see why God would be hurt, disappointed, and heartbroken that I had turned away from the best thing he had ever given me, to indulge in shallow and unfulfilling substitutes. I had disdained his gift. I had rebelled against his plan in order to pursue my selfish indulgence. I had treated the wife he gave me, which was the best a man could have, as if she had little value or meaning to me.

What would a father think if he gave his son a new Jaguar for graduation, and the boy drove it a few times and then parked it on the street and stole a souped-up Chevy for a joy ride? The father would be heartbroken, just as God was heartbroken at David's decisions.

King David came to realize how he had hurt God, and he repented. "I recognize my rebellion," David prayed, "It haunts me day and night. Against you, and you alone, have I sinned" (Psalm 51:3–4). The king knew he had committed offenses toward others, but his selfish taking demonstrated a breach of trust with his gracious and giving God. That was the most egregious offense. David came to realize that he didn't trust God with his needs and instead selfishly took what didn't belong to him. When that understanding dawned on David, he had reached a place of true repentance.

As Barbara was battling cancer and going through her emotional recovery process, God slowly but surely taught me the true meaning of confession and repentance as well. I began to understand a little of the magnitude of pain that my selfishness in the past had caused God as well as Barbara.

God could not have given a man any better wife than he gave to me. Barbara was devoted to me. She was always there for me. And what did I say to God when I was unfaithful to her? Without consciously realizing it, I said what King David said: "God, I don't trust you to meet my needs in your good timing. Therefore, I will selfishly take what doesn't belong to me and count your care and provisions as worthless." How that must have wounded the heart of God! He had done so much for me, yet I responded with unconscionable ingratitude, disrespect, and lack of trust.

When I realized what I had done to God, it broke my heart that I had broken his. That was what ultimately led me to repentance. The last thing I wanted was to hurt the God who had always been faithful to me. I didn't deserve his grace, yet he continually offered it. His patient and merciful love was overwhelming. My heart became broken and repentant.

That broken and repentant heart toward God was the fertile ground that would bear fruit as I approached Barbara. God was readying me to understand emotionally and experientially what Barbara had suffered because of me.

I Was Hurting Barbara

Slowly my mind and heart were being prepared for a new level of relationship with Barbara. I had begun to understand what my selfish unfaithfulness had done to my marital relationship. God meant for me to be the kind of gift to Barbara that she was to me. I was to be his gift to her, providing her with all the joy, fulfillment, and completion that God offered to me through her.

I had taken these gifts that God had wrapped for Barbara, to be delivered through my relationship with her, and had doled them out to other women and even to insentient printed and digital images with which I had no intimate relationship. It was, in effect, throwing God's pearls to swine. I was robbing Barbara of something God meant for her. My affections and sexuality were given to me to be directed toward her as a means of bonding us together. It crushes me even now to think of how my theft of that gift cheated her out of the joy God entrusted to me for delivery to her.

Consider this story: In past centuries when dowries were common, a young man became engaged to a fine and beautiful girl. Shortly before the wedding, her father delivered a dowry in cash to the young man, saying, "I started saving this when my daughter was born. I want her to have the finest wedding, the finest wedding dress, and the finest home this money can buy. And what I'm giving you is enough to buy her the very best." Then on the way to deliver the money to his fiancée, the young man turned aside to a gambling house and lost every penny of the dowry. That is much like what we do to our wives when our sexual attention strays. We squander riches that God entrusted to us to be delivered to our wives for their joy and emotional security.

Throughout the Bible, God makes it clear that he designed sex to be expressed exclusively between a committed husband and wife. Research shows that porn undermines that exclusivity. "Partners feel betrayed when they discover that their partner has been viewing pornography, which is perceived as infidelity."[12] Wives report feeling less intimate with husbands who indulge in porn. They "described their partner's sexual advances as conveying a message of objectification as opposed to meaningful interaction."[13]

My porn use not only destroyed Barbara's trust in me and fueled her sense of betrayal, it also made her feel that she wasn't enough in and of herself to satisfy my needs. She felt that she could not measure up to porn stars with their perfect bodies and the supercharged libidos they projected. Consequently, her sense of worth took a further nosedive. My porn use definitely hurt Barbara and hindered the opportunity for us to enjoy a deepened relational intimacy.

You might sum it up by saying that I finally learned the answer to the question posed in the title of this chapter. What's love got to do with it? Everything! Sex is not merely a side-benefit to love; sex is to be bound up in love. In the marriage relationship, love and sex are woven into a single fabric. Author Dr. Juli Slattery makes this point powerfully clear in her watershed book *Rethinking Sexuality—God's Design and Why It Matters*. (See more about her book in the appendix.)

In a healthy relationship, love should generate sex, and sex should generate love. But one must not get the cart before the horse, as I had done throughout my misguided life. Love comes first. Love must be present for sex to be all God meant it to be. Love enhances sex by allowing each partner to focus on giving the other pleasure simply because people who love always seek the other's wellbeing. That is loving as Jesus loves.

Slowly but surely, God brought me to a place where I understood more fully how my thought life and behavior hurt him, hurt Barbara, and hurt me. And he was about to give me the perfect opportunity to let Barbara know that I now comprehended the deep pain I had caused her.

Barbara was journaling and getting in touch with the hurts from her childhood, yet she was fearful of how I would react if she began to share her true feelings with me. But slowly she found the courage to unveil those feelings by opening her journal to me, which revealed what feelings she was getting in touch with. Then it happened.

On a December afternoon while on vacation, she mustered up the courage to share an entry from her journal that she had posted that morning. It touched on my past sexual indiscretions. I guess I shouldn't have been surprised by what she had written, but it did take me back a bit.

What happened next was truly extraordinary, even supernatural. It was something neither Barbara nor I ever expected!

12

Feeling Safe Enough to Be Real with Steve

Barbara's Journal: December 14

> *I looked at one of those sex books that happened to be on the table this morning— something about how to be a better lover. And I'm feeling inadequate sexually, like I'll never be able to please my husband...*

We were vacationing and Steve had brought a couple of books on sexuality, which were lying out on the coffee table. They caught my eye, and I made the journal entry cited above.

I need to make it clear that this entry was made years after Steve had stopped seeing call girls and viewing porn. He had long since apologized for his unfaithfulness, and I believed I had forgiven him. Furthermore, I had already begun to experience positive changes in Steve's attitude toward me—more concern, more love, and more care. Yet those books seemed to rise up and call forth Steve's indiscretions from the past to make me feel inadequate sexually in the present. It was so frustrating! The past would not let me go. I could not break free from the past to experience deep emotional and sexual intimacy with my husband in the present.

By now I had been through enough of my journey to know what I needed to do, but I remained reluctant to take the step. That fact is revealed in the rest of what I wrote in my journal on that December morning:

> I'm feeling threatened by the focus on sex—not sure why. I guess I haven't been able to be open and honest yet. I know in my head that Steve loves me more than ever and I wonder why I don't emotionally feel his love unconditionally yet.
> I guess I need to tell him how I'm feeling or it will never get better. But for so many years I was afraid of telling Steve how I was feeling—I was afraid of losing him. I can't stop crying.

This entry makes it clear that by now I knew that the healthy thing to do was to share these feelings openly with Steve. But despite what I had learned about God's love and acceptance, and despite positive changes I was seeing in

Steve, the thought of opening up frankly to him was still scary. Yet I was convinced that he needed to know I was struggling with feelings of inadequacy. He also needed to understand how afraid I was to share those feelings with him. I knew that unless I took this difficult step, Steve and I would never enjoy the intimacy we both were longing for.

I had already found the courage to be open with God. My assurance of his love and the fact that he had begun to heal those wounds from my past finally gave me strength to face Steve with my struggles. The next day, I approached him and said, "Do you have a moment? I'd like for us to talk for a little bit."

"Sure," Steve responded. "What's up?"

"Well, when I saw those books about how to be a better lover lying on the table, it triggered a negative reaction in me."

"A book about sex triggered a negative reaction? What do you mean?"

"I guess I'm afraid I'll never be able to please you sexually."

Steve could sense my uneasiness in raising the issue, and he suggested we sit down and talk it through. With a voice filled with concern and reassurance, he said, "I want to hear you out and understand where this is coming from, even if it's from my own past failings. Take your time. I really want to know what you are feeling."

You cannot imagine how warmed and elated I felt when Steve responded with such empathetic concern. Our interaction that day became a defining moment for both of us. In the past when I made any reference to Steve's previous indiscretions, he would get a little irritated. He figured if those sins were forgiven, they ought to be forgotten. But not on this day. He sensed a vulnerability in me that reached into his heart.

I sensed that he could see pain mixed with fear in my eyes. Instead of feeling irritated, he felt moved to alleviate my fears and heal my wounds.

Tears formed in his eyes, and he asked me to share more. He listened as I managed to express the pain I felt from years of neglect, betrayal, inattentiveness, and aloneness. The more deeply he comprehended my hurt, the more deeply he was moved emotionally. Understanding the depth of pain he had neglectfully inflicted stirred him to offer an emotional, heartfelt confession that I never imagined I would hear.

As I tearfully expressed my grieving heart, Steve grieved with me. He embraced me with tears streaming down his face and again sought my forgiveness. As we wept, we sensed God weeping with us. At that moment something took place within me. I could sense my impenetrable prison within being breached. The power of God's grace was at work. The thick protective walls that kept me from feeling Steve's love and devotion began to crumble. It didn't all happen overnight, but stone by stone and bar by bar, the prison in which I had lived was coming down. I began to feel accepted and safe. The fear that had paralyzed my life was being expelled. It was just as Scripture says: "Love has no fear, because perfect love expels all fear" (1 John 4:18).

I began to open up more and more to Steve as he expressed his tender and understanding heart to me. Our sharing and weeping together in the presence of God that day bonded us together with a completeness we had never before experienced. The foundation was laid for building a trust in Steve much like the trust I had placed in God. As God drew us closer to him, he also drew us closer to each other. We were rediscovering each other, coming to know each other as we never had before.

As this bonding intimacy continued, something utterly unexpected happened: I turned on sexually. Throughout our marriage, I would have described myself as sexually compliant, often engaging in sex as if I was just fulfilling a duty. But now I was becoming emotionally involved in the act, even aggressive. I surprised myself, and Steve was even more surprised—and thrilled!

Perhaps I unwittingly expressed the natural connection between emotional and physical intimacy in something I said to Steve as we were casually talking together sometime after our breakthrough: *"Steve, I want you to know something. Now that I feel highly valued and safe in talking to you about anything, you have become incredibly attractive to me."* I looked at him as if I could have pounced on him at that very moment. The emotional connection spurred the physical connection, and like a spark touching gunpowder, it ignited a dynamic sex life that greatly enhanced our connectedness. Steve happily says, *"That's just one of the perks of inviting God into the marriage relationship."*

Because of my bottled-up past, I had lived a life paralyzed by fear. But learning to accept and feel the unconditional love of Jesus coming through Steve was now casting out that fear. I had struggled terribly with a sense of unworthiness that kept me from loving myself or feeling the love that God and Steve had for me.

What amazed me most about all these positive changes in our marriage was discovering what caused my sense of inadequacy to melt away like ice exposed to the sun. It wasn't complicated. It was simply my response to Steve's caring and tender heart. I couldn't get over how attentive and considerate he had become, and it prompted an overwhelming sense of gratefulness within me. God used that simplicity of gratitude to soften the prison walls of my heart so that Steve's love could break through and reach the real me.

My sense of unworthiness was being replaced by a grateful heart, which had opened me up to feel love fully for the first time in my life. It began with gratitude toward Jesus, who considered me valuable enough to die for and offered himself as a safe place for me to be real. Steve had also become a safe place, and his tender love empowered me to love him in the same way I loved Jesus. That meant the world to me.

I won't pull any punches. The pain and anguish I suffered through those long months of anxiety, adrenal stress disorder, chronic fatigue syndrome, PTSD, depression, cancer, and the ordeal of chemotherapy were horrible. Yet I don't regret it for one moment. I'm not saying I would ever want to repeat any of it or that I enjoyed it. But those trials, severe as they were, launched Steve and me on a journey toward intimacy that we likely would never have taken unless forced by such impelling circumstances. In that journey we found ourselves, each other, and the reality that Jesus wanted to be at the center of our love relationship. The result has been the kind of emotional connection that God intended for us from the beginning. *In that respect, I have considered my cancer a "gift."*

And what about the childlike Barbara? Here's one of my last journal entries (September 1) written to the childlike Barbara:

Adult Barbara to Childlike Barbara

Now Steve is beginning to love you unconditionally. So it will be easier to tell him what you want, what you need, and what you like. Now you can love him back and enjoy intimacy knowing your value is not based on your performance—being a good girl, doing whatever he wants, or trying to please him just to keep him from leaving. That takes a lot of energy. It will be much better to be yourself, to show him love, grace, mercy—all the fruits of the Spirit—not just to gain his love but to express your love to him.

That is what God wants from us—our love for him, not simply trying to live up to some standard, but just loving him as he has loved us. And then loving others as we are loved by him. How do you feel now?

Childlike Barbara

I feel grateful, accepted, loved, hopeful, and important.

Freed from her prison of fear and hurt, the child within me grew up to become a more healthy and mature adult. I am that more healthy and mature adult. In a sense, the childlike Barbara was a symbol of my inability to become a healthy, fully integrated person—my inability to become the real me I was meant to be.

I give a lot of credit for my growth journey to Linda. She was there to guide me through the process. And then there was Steve, who changed into a loving, sensitive, and caring husband. But the real credit goes to God, because he became an active partner in our marriage. So much so that I believe our marriage is now a three-way relationship. No longer are we merely a couple; with God we have become a trouple! I will let Steve explain more fully what that means in the next chapter.

13

We Became a "Trouple"

Today, I sometimes look at myself and wonder who I am. What happened to the old Steve? Who is this newcomer now living in his body? It's true that I have drastically changed. Now I can hardly recognize the person I was prior to Barbara's panic attacks and cancer. Back then I was far more cerebral than emotional. I could relate to a business problem, but I couldn't easily tune in to an emotional issue, especially a painful one.

But on this journey of relational intimacy with Barbara, I began to tune in to her, to feel what she felt. Even if those feelings were painful, I opened my heart to let them in because I wanted everything that was part of her to also be part of me. I even began to learn how to help her identify her painful feelings and then grieve those feelings with her.

Looking back, I think this ability to identify with Barbara's emotional pain began when I saw her endure the physical pain of her second cancer surgery. It was a training exercise of sorts, a first step toward helping me to get in touch with her emotional pain.

Nine months had passed since eighteen inches of Barbara's colon had been removed. The chemotherapy had successfully eradicated the cancer, and it was time to reverse the colostomy and reattach the remaining part of her colon to restore normal bowel function. This final surgery was very painful, and I wanted to be at her side in the hospital room all night.

The doctors told me that Barbara would be incoherent throughout the night and wouldn't even know I was there. They warned me that even in an unconscious state and on morphine, she would no doubt scream out in pain. And indeed, she did—repeatedly.

It was a nerve-wracking experience. I definitely got in tune with her physical pain. I wanted to provide comfort to her and relieve her of pain. Although I couldn't do that on a physical level, the experience deepened a longing in me to be of true comfort to my wife on an emotional and relational level.

As I sat in that dimly lit hospital room that night, I had time to reflect on many things concerning my relationship with Barbara and with God. I remembered Pastor Darryl's "one thing," which was to love Barbara as Christ loves me. As I mulled over my many subsequent sessions with the pastor, I remembered him saying that my love for Barbara and my love for God are inextricably tied together. I would never love

God as I should until I loved Barbara as I should. Or, to put it another way, the extent to which we love others is the extent to which we love God.

At first, that sounded like a catch-22. Or like a merry-go-round spinning too fast to jump on. I couldn't love God properly until I loved Barbara, and I couldn't love Barbara properly until I loved God. Where was I to start?

If you had asked me how I showed my love to God prior to Barbara's panic attacks and cancer, I probably would have said something like, "I show my love to God by reading the Bible, praying, going to church, giving tithes and offerings, obeying the commands of Scripture, trying to follow God's commands, etc." That answer might indicate some kind of connection with God, but it hardly reaches the central core of how we express our love to him. Even the most religious people of the New Testament, the scribes and Pharisees, were meticulously scrupulous about performing those visibly religious acts. But without pulling any punches, Jesus made it clear that these people neither loved God nor their fellow man (see Luke 11:42–52). Their religious acts were measurable, tangible performances that one could do and check off a list without ever involving the heart.

The problem with making these overtly religious acts the focus of our Christianity is that they are too self-enclosed, too narrow, too much a matter of "just me and Jesus." But that is how I saw my relationship to God. It was pretty much an exclusive two-person vertical relationship that could be graphically expressed like this:

God

Me

I talked to God in prayer and told him I loved him. And I knew that he loved me in return, despite my seriously flawed understanding of what loving God really means. To clarify the true meaning of loving God, Pastor Darryl directed me to the Scripture where a scribe asked Jesus to identify the greatest commandment. He answered, saying:

> 'And you shall love the Lord your God with all your heart, with all your soul, with all your mind, and with all your strength.' This is the first commandment. And the second, like it, is this: 'You shall love your neighbor [near one] as yourself.' There is no other commandment greater than these. (Mark 12:30–31 NKJV)

"I want to love God as I should," I told the pastor, "but I don't know how to love someone I can't see, hear, or touch. How do I go about loving an invisible God?"

"That's easy," he replied. "You love your neighbor who you can see, hear, and touch."

"But how does loving my neighbor help me to love God?" I persisted.

"Do you remember the story of the separation of the sheep from the goats that Jesus told in Matthew 25?" Pastor Darryl asked. "Jesus commended the righteous people because they had fed him when he was hungry, clothed him when naked, and visited him when he was sick or in prison. These good people were baffled at his words. They didn't remember ever seeing or helping Jesus in any of those needy conditions. Then Jesus told them, 'Assuredly, I say to you, inasmuch as you did it to one of the least of these My brethren, you did it to Me' (v. 40 NKJV)."

He didn't have to explain further. I got the point. "So when we love others, we are actually loving God."

"Bingo!" he replied. "By loving others—our brother, our neighbor, our spouse, or whomever—we demonstrate our love to God. The primary way we can express love to God is to love those whom He loves."[14]

It finally sank into my head. When we love our neighbor as ourselves, you might say that God "feels" that love. It delights him. He exults in seeing us love others as he does. Our love for others reaches his heart as love for him.

The apostles clearly understood the meaning of Jesus' command to love one another. It meant that when we love our neighbor as we love ourselves, we are in fact loving God. That's why the apostle Paul pointed out that the "whole law can be summed up in this one command: 'Love your neighbor as yourself'" (Galatians 5:14). James made the same point in James 1:27 and 2:8—that loving others is to be the primary focus of a follower of Jesus. Why? Because they understood that our love for others is how we demonstrate our love to God.

The apostle John made it crystal clear that "if we love each other, God lives in us, and his love is brought to full expression in us. ... And everyone who loves the Father loves his children, too" (1 John 4:12, 5:1). It dawned on me that when I unselfishly love Barbara, I am simultaneously loving God. Since God dwells in my wife, he mysteriously feels my love toward him when I express my love to her. In other words, you might well say that God receives joy and love from our marriage relationship. As we both love each other, he is being loved, and he feels it!

Some people seem to struggle with the concept that our love for others is the primary way we demonstrate our love for God. Former pastor and founder of Servant Leadership Network, Gaylord Enns, experienced this struggle. He explains how he came to grips with the concept in his book *Love Revolution*:

> As I lay on my bed, God was reminding me that because He now lived *in* those people who believed in Jesus, we would need to love Him in His place of dwelling— *in* those people who believed in Him. He was making Himself accessible to us *in* our brothers and sisters, but it would be impossible to love Him *in* them if we did not *love the brothers and sisters in whom He now lived!* It was only when we hugged them that God would feel the squeeze!
>
> The thing that came to my mind was the following words of Scripture:

If anyone says, "I love God," yet hates his brother, he is a liar. For anyone who does not love his brother, whom he has seen, cannot love God, whom he has not seen. And he has given us this command: Whoever loves God must also *love his brother* (1 John 4:20–21).

In that moment, it seemed even clearer to me that God was deliberately positioning Himself so we could *only* love Him as we love our brothers and sisters *in whom He now lives.* If I don't love my brothers and sisters, it is impossible to "get to God" in order to love Him.

The words "cannot love God" seemed extremely significant to me in that moment. More important than my screaming toward the stars in the night sky, "I LOVE YOU, GOD!"—He was asking me to love my brothers and my sisters who were standing right next to me on planet earth. In so doing *I would be loving Him, too, as He now made His home in them.*

To me, it seems the way God best receives love from us is through our *obedience* to Him. When we obey His Command to love one another, we give God a double hug—the hug of obedience and then the hug He feels when we love those in whom He now makes His home. Because God now lives in those who believe in Jesus, He can't help but feel the squeeze when we love one another.[15]

I finally realized that the overarching, impelling, and continually active dynamic of the entire flow of love begins with God. It is his love for us that provides the fuel for the entire process. I can love Barbara with an unselfish, serving love only because I receive it first from an unselfish, serving God. In loving each other, we are all conduits of God's love. John said, "This is real love. It is not that we love God, but that he love[s] us. … We love each other as a result of his loving us first" (1 John 4:10, 19 NLT*).

As Barbara and I receive and accept God's love for us, we are empowered to love each other with his love. The result? God feels loved and is blessed by our marriage. My love for God is no longer just a vertical relationship between him and me. Nor is my love for Barbara merely a horizontal relationship between the two of us. Rather, my love for God and Barbara is a cyclical relationship involving God, Barbara, and myself, all loving one another.

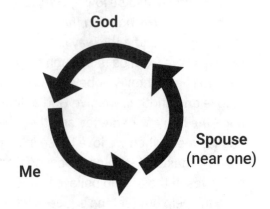

In a real sense we are no longer a couple; we have become a "trouple"—Barbara, myself, and God. Really, that's a word, albeit in the Urban Dictionary. It references a couple having another person who is always with them. There is no question now that God is always there in our relationship, giving and receiving our love. Wise Solomon gave credence to the state of a third person being in a relationship when he said, "Two people can accomplish more than twice as much as one. ...Three are even better, for a triple-braided cord is not easily broken" (Ecclesiastes 4:9, 12 NLT*).

When Barbara and I love each other with Jesus' unselfish, serving love, it creates a cycle of perfect love—Jesus loves the two of us, we love each other, Jesus feels loved by both of us, Jesus continues to love us, we continue to love each other, Jesus continues to feel loved by us, and on and on the cycle of perfect love continues into eternity.

I would like to take credit for the transformation that occurred in our marriage, but I can't. Sure, I was trying to love Barbara as Jesus loves her, but I couldn't do that on my own. It took the Holy Spirit loving through me to accomplish the kind of love that Jesus gives. I think this truth dawned on me that day on Maui as I truly sought forgiveness from Barbara. It was as if the Holy Spirit entered the room that day and enveloped the two of us within his arms. I am now convinced that he had been there through the entire conversation. In fact, I believe it was he who had supernaturally empowered me to confess and comfort Barbara then and who has repeated that empowerment many times since.

It was then that I began to realize that we were in the middle of a three-way relationship—a triune relationship consisting of Barbara, Steve, and God. Prior to this break-through, it seemed impossible for me to find the key to healing the wounds I had inflicted on Barbara. My apologies never seemed to do much, and no amount of compensatory acts had any effect. But when I got in touch with Barbara's pain, God was there in his mercy and grace to bring comfort and healing through us and to us.

The infinite scope of God's love is still difficult for me to grasp. The absolute, perfect, and holy God of the universe desires to wrap his arms around two broken people like Barbara and me. He wants to be in our relationship despite how much we have failed or how badly we were broken and wounded. It seemed to us that he was saying, *I am here loving you in the midst of your failures and brokenness. I will always be here with my relentless love. I will continue to wrap my arms of grace around the two of you to bring the three of us increasingly closer together.*

God's love and grace coming into the midst of our marriage was as surprising to me as it was amazing. Here he was, showing up to enable Barbara and me to experience a depth of healing, forgiveness, and deepened intimacy we could never have imagined.

People sometimes ask us how our marital transformation actually took place—in other words, how did we do it? In the last two chapters, Barbara and I will explain the salient points about what worked for us and, in fact, has worked for many other couples as well. Based on our experiences and our study, we partnered with Dr. David and Teresa Ferguson to create a guide to the primary factors that produce deepened marital intimacy. It's entitled *Called 2 Love: A 40-Day Journey into Marriage Intimacy,* and it is a transformative process that will enrich the best of marriages. (See the last pages of this book for a brief description of this resource.)

Regardless of where your marriage is right now, you can take it to another level—to a deeper, more intimate relationship. That is the beauty of a love journey between two people: no matter how broken it is or how good it is, it can keep getting better.

14

Be A.W.A.R.E. of the Process

"Well, tell me about your week," the counselor began as the couple settled into their chairs for their weekly counseling session.

"It happened again," Marci blurted out as she threw her hands up in disgust. "Chad wouldn't face up to the fact he hurt me this week. Just like last time, he had another excuse for being mean to me."

"Did you try to talk it through?" the counselor asked.

"I tried," Chad responded, "but Marci said she wouldn't discuss it until we met with you. And if you—"

"That's not true," Marci interrupted as she glared at Chad. "You wouldn't even listen to me, and there's no way we can resolve our problems if you're not going to listen to me."

"Okay, let's calm down," the counselor said. "Chad, why don't you tell us what happened."

"Well, we had some friends over Friday night," Chad began, "and someone mentioned something about another couple who's having trouble in their marriage. Then Marci speaks up ..." Chad hesitated as if questioning whether he should share his story.

"Okay, go on," the counselor said.

"Well, Marci begins telling our friends how I got ticked off because she deleted the football game from my DVR."

"Our DVR," Marci said.

"Whatever," Chad retorted. "The point is, she put me down in front of our friends. And when I confronted her about it after they left, she claimed I was at fault for being upset over her deleting a game I had recorded to watch. She said I should have admitted I was wrong in front of everyone. I was so humiliated. Whether I was right or wrong, she shouldn't be exposing our dirty laundry to everyone."

"Do you feel Chad has a point here, Marci?" the counselor asked.

"Absolutely not!" Marci replied. "The problem in our marriage is Chad, and he won't admit it."

"Chad has admitted he has problems," the counselor said, "but can you see how he might feel humiliated when you told your friends about his angry outburst?"

"I don't like where this is going," Marci responded. "Come on, Chad. We're leaving."

Marci left. After a brief pause, Chad followed, and they never met with the counselor again.

That's a true account of a couple unwilling to acknowledge their issues or place themselves in loving accountability to each other. Today their marriage continues to suffer, and their search for intimacy remains elusive. They are truly an unhappy couple.

I (Steve) was a lot like Marci. I hated to be wrong, and if anyone suggested I was, I either got defensive or avoided discussing the subject altogether. Because Barbara rarely resisted or disagreed with me, everything went along smoothly on the surface of our marriage. All the while, however, inner tension, fears, and pain were festering inside Barbara, building up pressure that emerged in her panic attacks.

Being human, we are all naturally inclined to defend and justify ourselves. But that inclination works against experiencing and maintaining an intimate connection with another person. My self-centeredness and self-defense mechanisms encouraged Barbara to remain closed. It was only when I was willing to stop pointing my finger at her and take full responsibility for my actions that she started to feel safe enough to open up and speak out.

Both Barbara and I needed to change the way we interacted with each other. And this is where the difficulties, troubles, and crises of life became our friends. Barbara's health issues tested us both. They created a crisis that told us we needed a major course correction in our relationship.

The change in me didn't happen quickly; it was a process. As I worked my way through the process, I discovered five key steps that moved me from a position of self-focus to one of true intimacy. Barbara and I both locked onto this process, which we call A.W.A.R.E. That's an acronym for the relationship-discovery journey we took in pursuit of knowing and loving each other and becoming more relationally intimate.

And it has worked wonders for both of us. Here's what we did—and still do:

Acknowledge we have problems and issues and place ourselves in accountability to each other.

Work with our story of brokenness to better understand why we do what we do.

Agree with God about our condition and turn to him as our change agent.

Rely on the Holy Spirit to enable us to love each other as Jesus loves.

Empower change as we develop new habits and patterns of behavior.

By going through the program in *Called 2 Love: A 40-Day Journey into Marriage Intimacy*, you will be guided through this process and offered much more information on achieving marriage intimacy.

Aware:

Acknowledge that I have problems and issues and place myself in accountability to my near one—my spouse.

I didn't want to acknowledge I had problems or was the problem for two reasons. First, it would show that I was wrong about something, and I hated being wrong. Second, admitting that I had problems would show that I was weak, and being thought of as weak was humiliating to me.

I learned, however, that admitting I had problems was not an admission of weakness; it was an expression of much-needed humility—a step toward overcoming the entrenchment of pride. And taking that step was a good thing. Wise Solomon said:

> Pride leads to disgrace, but with humility comes wisdom. (Proverbs 11:2)

> Fear of the LORD teaches wisdom; humility precedes honor. (Proverbs 15:33)

> True humility and fear of the LORD lead to riches, honor, and a long life. (Proverbs 22:4)

It's true, admitting I was wrong and in need of help was humbling. Yet the path I was on included learning to love my wife with a servant kind of love, and that in itself required humility. Peter said, "All of you serve each other in humility, for 'God opposes the proud but favors the humble'" (see 1 Peter 5:5).

My problem was that I associated neediness with weakness. I soon learned that this simply isn't the case. I discovered that relational and spiritual growth requires that I admit I am weak and in need. Admitting my imperfection opened me up to receive the perfect solution.

Jesus said, "God blesses those who realize their need for him" (Matthew 5:3 NLT*). Admitting my neediness was a path of blessing, and in my acknowledged weakness I could find strength. In practical terms, I turned to God and to Barbara for strength and help. And that strength and help came as I placed myself in account to both of them.

I told you, in an earlier chapter, of my desire to love more like Jesus. To bring this desire to fruition, I began a self-assessment program. I started by sitting down on Sunday afternoons and reviewing my week to *heighten my awareness* of my progress and my failures. Was I unselfishly loving Barbara or following my natural tendency toward being self-centered? I repeatedly read the definition of love from 1 Corinthians 13:4–6, and personalized the passage by substituting my name for the word love each time it was used. Then I recalled different events that had occurred in the week and asked myself whether or not:

Steve was patient.

Steve was kind.

Steve was not jealous or boastful or proud or rude.

Steve did not demand his own way.

Steve was not irritable and he kept no record of being wronged.

Steve did not rejoice about injustice but rejoiced whenever the truth won out.

I asked God to help me be that kind of loving person to Barbara during each day of the week. I admitted that in my weakness I couldn't do it on my own. I consciously made myself accountable to God and asked him to empower me to love as he loves. I knew that as a child of God, he "has given [me] his Spirit as proof that [I] live in him and he in [me]" (1 John 4:13), and "as the Spirit of the Lord works within [me], [I] become more and more like him and reflect his glory even more" (2 Corinthians 3:18 NLT*).

I not only needed God; I needed Barbara as well. I needed her to hold me in loving accountability. She knew my struggles and weaknesses, and I needed her to help me evaluate and measure how I was doing.

I conducted these self-examinations every week. But about every six weeks, I ventured to ask for Barbara's input on my progress: "How am I doing in the area of being patient and kind? How am I doing in the area of not demanding my own way? How am I doing in the area of not being irritable?" etc. I asked her to rate me in these areas using a scale of 1 to 10. I wanted to know how Barbara was actually experiencing my love toward her. At first, she was hesitant to rate me, but I insisted, "I need to know how I'm coming across. I can't see myself clearly. You are my mirror that lets me see how I'm doing."

I admit that I didn't get high scores when we first started this process. Neither did Barbara. But each time after rating each other, we always asked how we could do better. As a result, over time we both became sensitive to each other's relational needs and began to meet them more effectively.

Barbara and I were sitting in the Los Angeles airport one day, having just deplaned from a fifteen-hour flight from Singapore. Out of nowhere Barbara said, "It seems to me that there's been a role reversal."

My ears perked up in curiosity.

"You serve me so frequently," she continued, "it's almost as if you are my personal assistant."

What a gratifying affirmation of my progress! Acknowledging my problems and placing myself in account to Barbara was bringing about a definite change in me.

aWare:

Work with our story of brokenness to better understand why we do what we do.

How did I become a workaholic? Why did I always feel I had to be in control of things?

How did Barbara become such a people-pleaser? Why did she avoid conflict like the plague? Why did she tend to feel so unworthy and keep people from getting too close to her emotionally?

Questions like these are naturally uncomfortable because they indicate we have problems in our lives. But every human being is broken or dysfunctional in some way. No one has ever been born perfect, except one, and he was God incarnate. For the rest of us, it's just a matter of varying degrees of brokenness. If we don't acknowledge our problems and work with our story of brokenness, we become our own worst enemy. As soon as Barbara and I were able to accept the truth about our imperfections and understand our story of brokenness, we were on our way to recovery.

My story included a mean mother and a father who inadvertently taught me that my doing was more important than my being. As I indicated earlier, I was being programmed to find acceptance and love through what I could do. I became performance driven. That meant I attempted to find my value and worth as a person in what I did. I felt a deep and urgent compulsion to achieve and accomplish something to gain acceptance, especially from my father. To achieve that goal, I felt I had to control my environment. My greatest fear was the fear of failure. My highest relational needs were acceptance, security, and affection.

Barbara's story included a mother who forbade all expression of negative emotion and a father who left her. Emotionally, she was programmed to bury her pain and cover it up by being a "good girl." She became a doer and a people pleaser so others wouldn't reject her. She felt that she had to comply with what others wanted. Her greatest fear was the fear of abandonment. Her highest relational needs were attention, approval, and comfort.

Understanding our top relational needs and our respective stories of brokenness was crucial to our healing. It began to help us make sense of why I became a workaholic and a control freak and why Barbara couldn't feel emotions fully or let anyone come deeply into her life.

To top it off, we discovered that practically none of our broken and dysfunctional behavior came out of a conscious decision to act that way. I don't say this to make an excuse for wrong behavior. But the reality is that most of our actions come from subconscious programming that starts at conception and continues through our growing-up years.

Neuroscientists who study the brain say that between 95 and 99 percent of all our emotional responses come from our unconscious, learned behaviors. We don't have to consciously think about being selfish, envious, jealous, fearful, unworthy, impatient, or irritable when we don't get our way. We act in those ways out of our subconscious, self-protective nature. Many of these natural responses work primarily on the basis of our brain being programmed out of our past brokenness.

My drivenness to achieve and accomplish was programmed into me by my attempt to gain acceptance from my father. Fear of failure was deeply engrained within me. If anything got in the way of achieving success, this inadvertent programming subconsciously set off signals of anger.

It was almost the opposite with Barbara. She was programmed from childhood to shut down her own desires and feelings and comply with whatever plan was presented in order to avoid conflict. Fear of abandonment was so deeply engrained in her that her subconscious programming set off signals of compliance in the face of every potential conflict. She couldn't express negative emotions or assert her own desires.

It's not that we don't have the power to choose differently. Nor are we totally controlled by a subconscious power that forces us, like a puppeteer, to do all the wrong things. Yet our past experiences have an inordinate influence over what we feel and what we do.

Neuroscientists explain that our brain is divided into two distinct hemispheres. The left hemisphere is dominated largely by reason and logic. It's where words and language are formed. Facts, math, and science are comprehended here. It is reality based. The conscious mind processes about forty bits of information per second.

The right hemisphere of the brain is more concerned with feelings, imagination, symbols, images, and intuition. It is emotionally based. Neuroanatomist Dr. Jill Bolte Taylor puts it this way:

> The right hemisphere is all about this
> present moment. It's all about right here,
> right now … what this present moment

looks like, smells like, and tastes like, what
it feels like, and what it sounds like. Our
left hemisphere is a very different place.
Our left hemisphere thinks linearly and
methodically. Our left hemisphere is all
about the *past* and it's all about the *future*.[16]

The conscious mind processes at forty bits of information a second, whereas the subconscious mind, the limbic
brain, processes something like 20 million bits per second!
It's no wonder that we find change so incredibly difficult. The
accumulated patterns of our mental physiology work against
change.

Understanding our story of brokenness and why we were
doing what we were doing was incredibly helpful to Barbara
and me. But the change we were looking for wouldn't happen
just because we now realized from where and from whom our
issues and brokenness originated. What we needed now was
a willingness to change and the power to make that change.

aw<u>A</u>re:

Agree with God about our condition and
turn to him as our change agent.

If our subconscious mind has been programmed with hurtful, fearful, condemning, or otherwise harmful experiences, it's no wonder that we have a proclivity toward broken and wrongful behavior. Then add to that the reality that we were all born with a sinful nature, and you can see why the process of changing one's behavior really gets difficult.

The apostle Paul lamented, "I know that nothing good lives in me, that is, in my sinful nature. I want to do right, but I can't. I want to do what is good, but I don't. I don't want to do what is wrong, but I do it anyway" (Romans 7:18–19). The great apostle recognized that for us fallen humans, trying to change by the power of our own efforts is futile. It cannot be done without divine help.

When I recommitted my life to Christ, I definitely experienced a change in whom I wanted to follow. I no longer wanted to be controlled or so powerfully influenced by my subconscious, natural nature. The Holy Spirit had taken up residence in me, and he was there to redirect and refocus my life. Paul put it this way: "Let the Holy Spirit guide your lives. Then you won't be doing what your sinful [natural] nature craves" (Galatians 5:16).

The problem was that I still struggled with my subconscious, natural nature—those unconscious learned behaviors—even though the Holy Spirit was there to guide me and give me Christlike desires. Paul characterized the struggle in this way: "These two forces [our natural nature and the Spirit-produced desires] are constantly fighting each other, so you are not free to carry out your good intentions" (Galatians 5:17). When Paul says we are not free to carry out our good intentions, he does not mean that change is impossible. He is simply acknowledging that it will be difficult because of the continuing inner conflict between our natural selves and our attempt to submit to the Holy Spirit.

In my research about change, I ran across the word plasticity. In the context of neuroscience, plasticity describes the capacity of the brain to be molded into new ways of responding. Our brains can literally form new neural pathways. This means they can be reprogrammed. Nora D. Volkow, MD, in an article for the Dana Foundation, summarizes a fact that's been repeated by dozens of researchers and scientists:

> Neuroscientists have steadily built the
> case that the human brain, even when fully
> mature, is far more plastic—changing and
> malleable—than we originally thought.
> It turns out that the brain (at all ages) is
> highly responsive to environmental stimuli
> and that connections between neurons
> are dynamic and can rapidly change within
> minutes of stimulation.[17]

This plasticity of the brain makes change physiologically possible, and the power of the Holy Spirit in our lives makes it doable. But often He must take drastic measures that shake up our mental furniture in order to set the stage for bringing about the needed changes. That's what He did with us.

For years I thought I was so set in my ways that I'd never change. Until cancer visited our home, I didn't really think I could change. But change I did! And so did Barbara. I can tell you that she is a changed woman after her bout with cancer. She has become vulnerable and has learned to express much of what she feels. Her subconscious mind has been changed from the tightly closed and carefully guarded closet it once was. She is more open now, more vulnerable, and tells you what she feels. Her brain has been reprogrammed. So has mine. My priorities have changed, and I am no longer such a driven man.

The change we have experienced has brought us to a point where we now enjoy each other, always want to be with each other, and find life to be so full of meaning and purpose in just loving one another. What a change in us and our home!

awaRe:

Rely on the Holy Spirit to enable us to love as Jesus loves.

As Barbara and I evaluate our journey toward deeper intimacy, it's not so much about what we've learned over these past years; it is more about "learning how to relearn." Our relational and spiritual growth didn't occur because we found a formula or a list of five or twelve steps to follow. It's been a journey of relearning how to discover God and one another.

This may seem too simplistic, but it really comes down to learning to know and love God and your spouse. As we've said before, the order in which we approach those two loves is vitally important.

I didn't realize how profound 1 John 4:19 is until I began to relearn how to love from God's perspective. John wrote,

"We love each other as a result of his loving us first" (1 John 4:19 NLT*). He loves us first. It is vitally important that this fact registers in our heads and our hearts. This means as I begin to know him, love him, and receive his love, I will be empowered to love as he loves.

The principle is simple: I can only give what I have received. You can't very well give away what you don't have. As I experientially receive Jesus' kind of love, I can love Barbara with that kind of love. As I allow him to love me, I can allow his love to flow through me to Barbara. This gives birth to the cyclical relationship of Jesus loving me, me loving Barbara, and both of us expressing God's love to each other as we love him in return. He loves us first; we receive it and pass it on.

I always felt a little unsure about how we are to actually be like Jesus and love as he does, until I grasped the truth that he is the one who gives us the power to be like him and love like him. The apostle Paul said to "imitate God" (Ephesians 5:1) and to "have the same attitude that Jesus Christ had" (Philippians 2:5). That seemed impossible for me to accomplish. How can a fallen human like me possibly love with the same attitude that Jesus, the perfect, sinless Son of God, had?

Paul understood this dilemma and made it clear how we can be like Jesus: "Imitate God, therefore, in everything you do, because you are his dear children. Live a life filled with [his] love, following the example of Christ" (Ephesians 5:1–2). Because I am his child, I can receive (be filled with) his love and pass it on to others. That allows me to love as he loves.

Something struck me as I read verses such as, "As we know Jesus better, his divine power gives us everything we need for living a godly life" (2 Peter 1:3 NLT*) and "You have clothed yourselves with a brand-new nature that is continually being renewed as you learn more and more about Christ" (Colossians 3:10 NLT*). It seems that knowing Jesus better and learning more about him is directly linked to being like him and loving like him. With this in mind, I began thinking of the Holy Spirit as my "Coach." He was someone who would be with me every day, someone I could get to know, someone who would give me direction and guidance.

Looking back, I can see that this awareness of the Spirit's continued presence with me was one of the most impactful lessons I learned. To this day I wake up saying, "Coach, what are we going to change today?" *By starting my day looking for change, I put myself in a receptive mindset for God to bring about a Christlike transformation.*

Don't think for one minute that I've got this mastered. I don't. But my, what a difference it is from the old way of trying to love in my own strength! When we rely on the Holy Spirit (our Coach) he "produces his fruit in our lives—love, joy, peace, patience, kindness, goodness, faithfulness, gentleness, and self-control" (Galatians 5:22–23).

awar<u>E</u>:

<u>E</u>mpower change as we develop new habits
and patterns of behavior.

Our new approach was making a real difference in our lives. Transformation was taking place. New habits were being programmed into both of us to replace the old unconsciously learned behaviors. We realized that something supernatural was occurring.

I would like to take credit for the transformation that was happening in our marriage, but I can't. Sure, I was trying my best to be patient, gentle, humble, kind, encouraging, forgiving, etc. But I couldn't grow those precious fruits of the Spirit on my own. All credit goes to the Holy Spirit, my Coach. He is the one who is patient, kind, humble, gentle, encouraging, and forgiving in his relationship to me. His love toward me is what empowers me to be loving to Barbara.

Scripture made that empowering reality so clear to me:

> May the Lord lead your hearts into full understanding and expression of the love of God and *the patient endurance that comes from Christ.* (2 Thessalonians 3:5)

> You are a *God of forgiveness.* (Nehemiah 9:17)

> Remember, *the Lord forgave you,* so you must forgive others. (Colossians 3:13)

> God in *his gracious kindness* declares us not guilty. (Romans 3:24 NLT*)

> Cry out for this nourishment, now that you have had a taste *of the Lord's kindness.* (1 Peter 2:2–3)

> Learn from me, for *I am gentle and humble in heart.* (Matthew 11:29 NIV)

In these passages I have italicized the phrases that describe the attributes of God that he passes on to me. When

I receive these attributes from him, he empowers me to model them to Barbara. They reinforce again and again that my "Coach," the Holy Spirit, is the change agent in our marriage. Barbara and I never want to forget that "unless the Lord builds a house, the work of the builders is wasted" (Psalm 127:1). He is the one who has rebuilt our house!

We are not the only ones who have discovered this process. Many leaders are awakening to the reality that change is needed and that change is possible. A movement of loving like Jesus is building across this country and around the world.

The last chapter of this book confirms this. Many people are connecting the dots as Barbara and I have done and putting the "Love Like Jesus" principle into action. We are beginning to see a rising movement that emphasizes loving as Jesus loves.

15

Connecting the Dots
That Put Love in Action

In the end, you could have all the money
you've ever wanted, a successful career,
and be in good physical health, but without
loving relationships, you won't be happy.[18]
— Melanie Curtin, 75-year Harvard study

The quote above sounds a lot like something the apostle Paul
said: "If I could speak all the languages of earth and of angels,
but didn't love others … If I had the gift of prophecy, and if I
understood all of God's secret plans and possessed all knowledge, and if I had such faith that I could move mountains, but
didn't love others, I would be nothing" (1 Corinthians 13:1–2
NLT). Paul clearly concluded that regardless of what accom-

plishments he accumulated, unless he loved others, his life would be without meaning and happiness.

Paul's conclusion mirrors that of the seventy-five-year Harvard study that followed 456 poor men growing up in Boston from 1939 to 2014, and 268 male graduates from Harvard's classes of 1939–1944. According to Robert Waldinger, director of the Harvard Study of Adult Development, one thing the study revealed surpasses all the rest in terms of importance: "The clearest message that we get from this seventy-five-year study is this: *Good relationships keep us happier and healthier. Period.*"[19]

If anyone wants humans to find happiness in loving relationships, it's God. He created us to glorify him by experiencing the joy of loving him and loving one another. If there's any group of people on earth that should be happy and enjoy loving relationships, it is those who love God with all their hearts. Yet that doesn't seem to be the case. Many Christian couples seem to be missing out on marital bliss.

Praise goes to the Southern Baptist Convention, the largest Protestant denomination in America, for conducting *their own research* a few years back, finding that divorce rates in their churches were higher than divorce rates in the demographic surrounding their churches. As a result, they unanimously passed a most remarkable resolution at their annual convention. Instead of trying to ignore the problem in an effort to maintain the public-relations fiction that Christians usually have exemplary marriages, they boldly confronted the issue head-on. They acknowledged "how damaging Southern Baptist accommodation to the divorce culture is to our global witness for Christ."[20] And they took steps to improve the quality and durability of marriage relationships in their churches.

Reports like that were in my mind when I had lunch one day with a friend, Bill Heitzman. During the conversation, I lamented, "Even with the plethora of books on marriage, small group DVD series, marriage seminars, and couples retreats available to us, today there is probably more strife in families than ever." I wondered out loud what we could do to facilitate genuine change that would make a difference in people's lives. What concerned me most was the reality that few Christians could tell us what makes a marriage emotionally meaningful and relationally intimate.

The Barna Group has conducted surveys among churched Americans over the past two decades that seem to confirm the condition found within the Southern Baptist study—that the lifestyles of professed born-again Christians are not much different from those who do not profess to be Christians at all.

Recently, an extensive survey commissioned by The Navigators and NavPress was conducted among 893 church leaders and over 2,000 adults professing Christianity. One of the goals was to determine the state of discipleship among American churches. There was a clear consensus among lay-people and church leaders as to what constituted a disciple of Christ. It was summarized in the phrase "becoming more Christlike."[21]

While today's church leaders see their responsibility as discipling people toward Christlikeness, it appears that few believe the church is accomplishing that directive. Only 1 percent of church leaders believe "today's churches are doing 'very well' at discipling new and young believers" into Christ-likeness.[22] And when pastors were asked to name the most critical elements of discipleship, aside from prayer and time with God, 94 percent said the top spiritual discipline toward discipleship was a "personal commitment to grow in Christ-likeness."[23]

While there appears to be a consensus among church leaders that discipleship is about growing into Christlikeness, a larger question remains: "What does Christlikeness look like in the life of a disciple of Jesus?" More specifically related to the subject of this book, what does Christlikeness look like to a Christian married couple?

While it may seem encouraging that the vast majority of Christian leaders and professed Christians believe Christ-likeness is a top priority, the problem lies in how they actually define what their commitment to Christlikeness should look like.

Of the pastors surveyed by the Barna Group, 75 percent couldn't define the process leading toward Christlikeness except to vaguely generalize it by saying, "Obey the teachings of the Bible."[24] The same Barna study revealed that 81 percent of professed Christians in America believe as these pastors do—that being discipled in Christ means "trying harder to follow the rules of the Bible."[25]

But Jesus never made "trying harder to follow the rules" of Scripture the main criteria for being his follower. Trying harder through obedience, discipline, and commitment doesn't characterize the biblical process of becoming a disciple of Christ. The "try harder" approach better describes the process followed by the Pharisees of Jesus' time. The religious leaders of his day focused on strict adherence to scriptural rules but showed little inclination to love their neighbors. This isn't to say that every church today follows the rulebound theology of the Pharisees. Not all do. But do you think perhaps the focus on trying harder and following God's law—a mode adopted by many people today—misses the heart of the Gospel, just as the Pharisees missed it? They had the head part right; we are to obey the commands of the law. But they missed it on the heart part; they failed to enter a heartfelt loving relationship with God or with others.

Jesus himself made the correct focus clear to his disciples. He said that the greatest commandment is to love God with our everything and to love our neighbor (our near one) as ourselves. Jesus lived a life of other-focused love and commanded his followers to imitate him: "This is my commandment, that you love one another as I have loved you" (John 15:12 ESV). His own definition of being like him is to love like him.

Being discipled into Christlikeness is best understood in a loving marital relationship as two people growing into an increasingly deepened connection of oneness. Jesus prayed that he and his followers, the church, would enjoy oneness as he did with his Father. "I pray that they will all be one, just as you and I are one—as you are in me, Father, and I am in you. … May they experience such perfect unity that the world will know that you sent me and that you love them as much as you love me" (John 17:21, 23).

Our earthly marriages actually bear the spiritual image of a loving, intimate relationship between the Father, the Son, and the Holy Spirit. That love connection leads to a relational intimacy that the outside world hungers for. That kind of loving is what actually draws people to Christ. Marriage as God designed it is a microcosm of what he wants his church to be. When a group of married couples love God and their closest neighbor as themselves, they put Christ's bride on display to the world around them.

A marriage between a man and a woman isn't characterized by a set of rules they follow but by an ever-deepening love relationship between the two of them. In a similar way, we are identified as disciples of Jesus by loving as he loves, not by the religious activities we engage in or the rules we follow. As Jesus said, "By this all people will know that you are my disciples, *if* you have love for one another" (John 13:35 ESV, emphasis added). Rule-keeping and religious activity do not draw people to Christ; it is our love for one another that makes authentic Christianity so appealing and attractive.

Imagine dozens of married couples—all loving each other as Christ loves them—worshipping and fellowshipping together. When they encounter difficulties and conflicts, they see them as opportunities to change and grow in Christlikeness. What would the outside world think and say about a community of couples like that? Most likely they would say, "I'd like to hang around with that crowd in hopes that some of what they've got will rub off on me."

What happens when a loving couple enjoys physical intimacy over time? Most often, a replica of the couple is born. Physical intimacy naturally leads to human reproduction. So it is with a community of couples loving like Jesus. Love for one another is an act that can naturally reproduce new born-again Christians. When Christian marriages are healthy, the church is healthy and grows both in numbers and in spiritual maturity.

In some respects, this principle seems so simple. At least it did to me. God loves you unselfishly, and you love him and those around you with his kind of unselfish love. That is the Great Commandment in action, which in turn results in Christlikeness. If married couples within the church would start loving each other with God's kind of love, every church community would be "like a city on a mountain, glowing in the night for all to see" (Matthew 5:14 NLT*).

This vision of Christian marriages reflecting Christ's relationship with his true bride, the church, got me so excited that I coordinated an investigative group composed of thirty-two ministry leaders from around the country. I posed to them this two-pronged question: "What is change, and what would bring it about?" If marriage relationships are going to improve, obviously something has to change. So what can be done to get more married couples to change and love like Jesus?

I asked these leaders to read our six key books on change and rank their top ten observations from each book. To be honest, I was a little disappointed and somewhat frustrated with the response. I had hoped these leaders would reflect a consensus. I was looking for a unified and clear plan of action that would dramatically improve the health of Christian marriages and thereby improve the health of the church. I wanted to see an increase of couples loving and growing in Christlikeness.

But such a plan was not forthcoming from these responses. What seemed clear to me didn't seem that clear to others. Yes, these church leaders acknowledged and lamented the fact that Christians' professions of faith didn't necessarily mean transformed lives. But most of them saw no clear way to reverse that trend. I was disappointed in the response, but shortly afterward I discovered that some prominent church leaders had made a thorough study of this problem—a study that revealed some startling observations.

Ten years prior to the challenge to my investigative group, the megachurch Willow Creek Community Church in the Chicago area began a process to discover their effectiveness in making Christlike disciples. Their extensive research led them to the conclusion that they had been working from the wrong assumption for thirty years. They had assumed that if people participated in the programs and activities of the church, they would experience spiritual maturity—which they defined as being conformed to the likeness of Christ. They concluded that their assumption had been woefully misguided!

The news of Willow Creek's findings spread throughout many evangelical churches. Some began to reevaluate how they were discipling their people. They discovered that following the programs and rituals of religion is not transformative. It does not empower a person to love like Jesus. Paul warned Timothy that people who merely follow the forms of godliness will lack the power to change (2 Timothy 3:5).

Willow Creek's findings led them to offer other churches the same survey materials that they used to measure the spiritual state of their church. To date, over 850 churches have conducted the same research, involving over 235,000 congregants among more than 12 denominations in America.[26] The results reflected the essence of Paul's warning. They were following the forms of religion but lacked the power to change.

The Willow Creek Association (WCA) determined that 5 percent of the 850 churches surveyed did the most effective job of challenging their people to love like Christ. From this top 5 percent of churches, however, only 25 percent of their members were satisfied with the church's role in their spiritual growth. Of the remaining 95 percent of churches, only 15 percent of their people said the church was doing a good job of discipling them to be like Christ.[27] The implication was that 75 to 85 percent of all evangelical churches were failing to disciple their members in Christlikeness.

These findings sounded a wake-up call to many church leaders. The WCA study was specific enough in its examination to make it apparent that a profession of faith in Jesus doesn't automatically lead people to love like Jesus. The 235,000 professed Christians were carefully surveyed to identify those who considered themselves truly Christ-centered. When asked their level of agreement with the statement, "I love God more than anything else," 78 percent said they "very strongly agree." Of course, it's understandable that more spiritually mature people would naturally declare their deep love for God.

But what is surprising is that these "spiritually mature" Christians seemed to have a disconnect between loving God and loving others. The study revealed that the *most mature* Christ-followers reported "love of others" *lower than any other segment in the study*. The researchers stated that while the Christ-centered people are fired up with their "love of God," their "love of others" trails far behind.[28]

How could this be? Wouldn't you think that husbands and wives who say they love God more than anything else would also be those who love each other intimately? How could a Christ follower's sincere love for God not translate into a compassionate love for others? How can people say they truly love God yet not feel a deep concern and love for their closest neighbor?

It began to dawn on me why many marriages among professed Christians are hardly any different from those of non-Christians. Their own love for God isn't being translated into a deep love for their closest neighbor, their spouse. Such marriages clearly reflect a disconnect between loving God and loving others.

The WCA study and other factors have sounded a wake-up call to church leaders around the country. Church after church has begun to reemphasize the importance of loving others as we love ourselves without diminishing adherence to the truths of Scripture. As a result, we are beginning to see a movement of people toward loving as Jesus loved.

While it may seem that a lot of churches today are failing to make loving others a priority, this move could well reverse that trend. We want to give a voice to four church leaders who are at the forefront of this movement. They are encouraging people, especially married couples, to love like Jesus. These leaders realized early in their ministry how easy it is to misplace priorities regarding the love of others.

Internationally known speaker Josh McDowell, marriage speaker and writer Gary Chapman, Pastor Jeff Bogue, and relationship counselor David Ferguson began their ministries preaching a gospel message urging people to love God. But they soon realized they were failing to love their closest neighbor as they loved themselves, and they changed their lives accordingly. These four men have written powerful stories explaining what turned them around, and with their permission we include those stories below.

The first is from David Ferguson, director of the Great Commandment Network. With openness and vulnerability, he shares significant highlights from his own life of misplaced priorities. Today David is a vital champion of the Called 2 Love movement.

Where Great Commandment Love Begins

by David Ferguson

It had been a stressful yet fulfilling day for me, juggling a secular job and a demanding part-time ministry to students. My schedule had been packed with typical activities: an early morning discipleship group, a number of appointments throughout the day, paperwork, lunch with a church elder, several phone calls from students, and another round of tinkering with a faulty computer program. I left a pile of work on my desk at six p.m. to run home for a quick supper. Then I hurried off to the church for a counseling appointment and a committee meeting that would last until past ten.

As usual, Teresa and the children barely noticed that I had come and gone. They were accustomed to my brief appearances at home. But I prided myself on being diligent in both work and ministry, as evidenced by the long hours I put in.

By the time I got home late that night, Teresa was in bed but still awake. I slipped into bed beside her and turned out the light. We talked in generalities about the day. I described my accomplishments, and she related how the kids had behaved—and misbehaved—at home.

At this point in our marriage, our conversations were rather superficial, as was the rest of our relationship. I was so busy with my job and running a growing student ministry, and she was so busy running the home, that we rarely connected deeply with each other. I silently lamented the fact that Teresa was not more committed to the ministry, which I sometimes interpreted as a lack of commitment to me as well. We were not enemies, yet there was a distance in our marriage that was unsettling to me.

Staring up at the ceiling in the darkness, I addressed the issue. "Teresa, I sense a dryness between us, like we live on opposite sides of a big desert. We are so involved in our own separate worlds of activity that we hardly notice each other. Is this the way it's always going to be with us?"

There was silence on Teresa's side of the bed, followed by a deep sigh. "I don't know, David."

Finally, I found the courage to ask the question that had been haunting me for months. "Teresa, do you really love me?"

Silence again. When Teresa finally answered, I was not prepared for the directness of her response. "David, I don't feel anything for you. I'm just ... numb."

The words stung my heart. I didn't know what to say. I knew there was some distance between us, but she was talking about a complete lack of love.

Ever since becoming a Christian, I had been trying to strike a workable balance between my family, my work, and my ministry commitments. Up until that moment in the bedroom, I thought I was doing a pretty good job. In the wake of Teresa's sobering statement, I was more confused than ever about love, relationships, and God's plan for ministry. To be honest, I did not know the first thing about sharing God's true love with those dearest to me. I was deeply committed to the ministry, for I would soon become a full-time associate pastor at the church. But I also desired the intimacy of a devoted wife and loving children. With Teresa's loveless words echoing painfully in my heart, it appeared that I might be on the verge of being denied both.

At the time, I thought the dry distance in our marriage was rare among ministry couples. But as Teresa and I interact with thousands of couples and single adults in Christian leadership every year, I see that our painful struggle with priorities is not at all uncommon. Many Christians in ministry have misplaced priorities related to family relationships and ministry. In fact, the vast majority of church pastors claim their ministry has a negative effect on their families. This shouldn't be the case.

We have also observed that countless single adults in Christian leadership minister to the multitudes while struggling with a deep fear of intimacy in their own personal relationships! These findings are staggering. Why does the call to love others produce such adverse results in the God-ordained relationships of marriage, family, and friendship?

I believe one major culprit is an insidious, destructive myth circulating among today's Christian leaders: the idea that we can achieve balance between ministry and family demands. We assume that the call to love family and the call to love ministry are separate and distinct, competing against each other for our attention.

These two roles are like two china plates a juggler spins at the top of long sticks. When pressures at church mount, we urge our families to "just understand, adjust, and be patient" while we give all our time and energy to keep the ministry plate spinning. When pressures at home mount due to neglect, we give the wobbling family plate a few frantic spins by repenting and canceling a few commitments in hopes that God and the family are satisfied. But we cannot keep both of them spinning successfully. Sooner or later, one of them will fall.

Trying to balance family and ministry runs contrary to the call of the Great Commandment to love. These seemingly conflicting roles are not like two fragile plates we must keep aloft and spinning. Family and ministry are two concentric circles surrounding an individual's personal relationship with God. Any public ministry God grants us should flow out of our love relationship with him and out of our loving ministry to family, friends, or other "nearest neighbors." In these nearest relationships we come to understand the practical aspects of Christian ministry. In them we learn both to live and to share God's concern for human fallenness and human aloneness. Living out the truth in our nearest relationships is the prerequisite for teaching the truth effectively in our ministry relationships.

Christian leaders and pastors all across the country are beginning to connect the dots. Many are convinced that the proclaiming of the gospel message—the Great Commission—is to be communicated largely through a lived-out message—the Great Commandment.[29]

***

My Misconception about Putting God First

by Josh McDowell

Early in my ministry, my wife Dottie traveled with me from city to city. She enthusiastically embraced my speaking ministry, and in many ways she was my partner in ministry. As we began to have children, it became difficult for her to be on the road with me. So she settled down in one place to make the "McDowell home" while I still kept a packed schedule of traveling all over the country.

Dottie was fine with this arrangement because she understood what my speaking ministry was all about. At the same time, raising a family while the husband and dad was out speaking wasn't easy. I remember at one point she shared how difficult it was beginning to be doing things on her own. I had told her to speak up anytime my schedule put too much of a strain on her. And she did.

I have to admit I struggled a little with my loyalties. I wanted to be there for Dottie while at the same time keeping God first in my life. How was I going to keep making him a priority in ministry and still attend to the needs of my family? I thought when push came to shove, he had to come first and my family second.

I'm sure glad I had chosen to make myself accountable to a few wise and more mature men at that time in my life, because they gave me wise counsel. I remember that my accountability partners helped me understand a few passages of Scripture about putting God first in my life.

The apostle Peter directed husbands this way: "You husbands must give honor to your wives. Treat your wife with understanding as you live together. ... Treat her as you should so your prayers will not be hindered" (1 Peter 3:7). Jesus said, "You must love the Lord your God with all your heart, all your soul, and all your mind ... [and] 'love your neighbor as yourself'" (Matthew 22:37–39). The apostle John wrote, "Let's not merely say that we love each other; let us show the truth by our actions" (1 John 3:18).

It took me back a little at first to think that if I didn't treat Dottie with honor and understanding, my prayers would be hindered. That was a big deal to me. I also realized that loving God with my everything was directly tied to loving my neighbor, and my wife was my closest neighbor. Finally, my love of Dottie couldn't just be words spoken on a long-distance call; I had to put my love in action.

Putting God first took on a whole new perspective for me. God didn't want Dottie and my family to come before my ministry; he wanted them to be my first ministry. Showing continued love and care to Dottie and the kids became a powerful platform to minister to others. Putting God first was actually lived out and expressed in loving and attending to my closest neighbor, my wife.

That perspective changed everything. I didn't stop traveling, but my speaking schedule took on a whole new dimension. It began to revolve around loving and caring for my wife and children first. Living with the woman I loved in an understanding way kept my prayers to God from being hindered. Together he, Dottie, and I began to make a great marriage! We still enjoy a great marriage. That isn't to say I still don't struggle with demonstrating my commitment to Dottie while maintaining a busy schedule—I do. But it makes all the difference in the world when I see that God wants me to love him with my everything and love my closest neighbor (Dottie) as myself.[30]

***

In a way similar to David and Josh, author and speaker Gary Chapman questioned how he could minister to others without having a healthy married life.

Problem in My Marriage

by Gary Chapman

My wife, Karolyn, and I have been "married and still loving it" for over five decades. We have walked together through sunshine and rain, through darkness and light. We have been open about sharing the struggles of the early years of our marriage. It was in those dark days that I often thought, I have married the wrong person. This is never going to work. We are too different.

I was in seminary at the time, studying to be a pastor, and the closer I came to graduation, the more I realized that I could never stand before people and preach a message of hope when I was so miserable in my marriage. I will never forget the day I finally said to God, "I don't know what else to do. I've done everything I know to do, and it is not getting any better."

As soon as I prayed that prayer, there came to my mind a visual image of Jesus on His knees, washing the feet of His followers. And I heard God say to me, "That is the problem in your marriage. You do not have the attitude of Christ toward your wife." It hit me like a ton of bricks because I remembered what Jesus said when He stood up having washed the feet of His disciples: "I am your leader, and in my kingdom, this is the way you lead."

I knew that was not my attitude. In the early years my attitude toward her was like, "I know how to have a good marriage. If you will listen to me, we will have one." She would not "listen to me," and I blamed her for our poor marriage. But that day I got a different message.

The problem was my own attitude was not Christlike, serving. So I said to God, "Lord, forgive me. With all of my study in Greek, Hebrew, and theology, I have missed the whole point." Then I said, "Please give me the attitude of Christ toward my wife."

In retrospect, it was the greatest prayer I ever prayed regarding my marriage, because God changed my attitude. Three questions made this practical for me. When I was willing to ask these three questions, my marriage radically changed. They are simple questions:

What can I do to help you?

How can I make your life easier?

How can I be a better husband to you?

When I was willing to ask those three questions, Karolyn was willing to give me answers. This was long before I knew anything about the five love languages, but essentially she was teaching me how to love her by serving her. When I began to be responsive to her answers, our marriage radically changed. Within three months she started asking me those three questions. We have been walking this road now for a long time, and I have an incredible wife. In fact, not too long ago I said to her, "If every woman in the world was like you, there would never be a divorce."[31]

***

Jeff Bogue, lead pastor of Grace Church in greater Akron, Ohio, also struggled with balancing ministry with family. In his book *Living Naked*, Jeff opens up and reveals the trouble he and his wife, Heidi, experienced over the role of church activity in their lives as he first began working in youth ministry.

My Misplaced Priorities

by Jeff Bogue

Youth ministry at the church was going extraordinarily well. We were seeing many kids deeply affected. In fact, our success was putting our youth ministry on the map. But "success" at home was less than extraordinary. When my son Josiah was born, Heidi and I found that raising a young child and running a large youth ministry came in conflict with each other, because the schedule of teenagers and the schedule of a baby are totally different. But I was committed to keeping God first in my life. Heidi couldn't be involved as much in the youth ministry because she was home with the baby. However, I worked in the ministry just as diligently as ever.

When I came home late in the evenings, often after dinner had been put back in the fridge and our child was in bed, I began to sense some sort of tension between Heidi and me. She was left alone while I was out ministering to others. She was exhausted, lonely, and frustrated.

Now you need to know something about Heidi: she is perhaps the most patient person on the planet. So when she finally reaches her limit, you know you have really achieved something. She didn't say much, but I knew something wasn't right. I shrugged off her apparent downer attitude as fatigue and took it in stride. That's what I had always done. When people weren't on board with me, I would just consider it their problem and move on. After all, I was putting God first in my life, and I couldn't let a wife's lack of enthusiasm hold me back from that.

By this time, I had added to my schedule traveling all over the country, speaking at youth events, and teaching youth ministry to college students. I was well received wherever I went. The more doors that opened, the more eager I was to plunge through them. Wherever I went, kids were ministered to, youth leaders were encouraged, and college students were instructed. I was convinced that God was totally in my ministry, because I was sacrificing myself and putting him first.

The more I was gone, however, the more tension and distance I felt growing between Heidi and me. And those feelings became more intense after our second son, Isaac, was born.

The turning point came when I spoke at a large youth event attended by many kids who had heard me at a previous event. Some of these kids had actually made buttons and T-shirts, proclaiming themselves to be my fan club. It was a great event. Hundreds of kids were affected, lives were changed, and I felt the Spirit of God move. What's more, I was now a celebrity!

I drove home in the middle of the night, basking in the glow of having served the Lord and having my own fan club. As I neared home, I called Heidi to see how she was doing. She replied that she was dog-tired, the kids were sick, and she really wanted me home. I listened to her, but soon moved the conversation to where I wanted it to be: on the Lord's work. I told her about the wonderful things God had done at this youth event, how teenagers would be forever changed because we were both sacrificing for God, and the bonus was that I now had my own fan club.

The conversation ended just as I pulled into the driveway. Heidi met me at the door and handed Isaac to me. He had just had a diarrhea explosion, and the fallout was dripping from his diaper. Josiah was in the kitchen throwing up. She half-jokingly said, "Welcome to reality, hot shot!" and then turned to go attend to Josiah.

Well, let me tell you, Heidi's attitude really got under my skin. After the boys were taken care of, I asked her, "What's with you? You don't seem to care that the ministry has gone so well and we're achieving the very dreams that we set out to achieve. I don't get your attitude."

Heidi looked at me and began to lay it out. She said she felt alone in the marriage. She told me she got little support or help from me in raising our sons. She explained she felt abandoned and dumped on with all the grunge work, while I simply used our home as a refueling and maintenance terminal to keep me flying high in my world of achievement.

She even had the audacity to ask, "Honey, is it really God you are seeking? Or is it about you and your ego and feeling fulfilled because you are 'effective in ministry'? If you really believe it is all about God, I'll pay this price and we will learn to live this way. But is this really what God wants?" She didn't say this in anger or with a whine. She was simply being open with me about how she felt. But the bottom line was clear: she felt that I valued my ministry more than I valued her.

My first impulse was to fling a Scripture or two at Heidi, reminding her to "seek God's kingdom first, and all these things will be added to you." But the more I heard the pain in her voice and saw the hurt in her eyes—pain and hurt that I had caused—the more I realized that God couldn't be pleased with the way I was treating her. Maybe I should help her more, but wouldn't that hinder me from putting God first in my life?

Then another Scripture verse came to me—the passage that describes the true nature of love. It says, "If I give all I possess to the poor and give over my body to hardship [be martyred for Christ's sake] that I may boast, but do not have love, I gain nothing" (1 Corinthians 13:3 NIV). I was sacrificing for God, and I was willing to even do more. But was love my real motivating factor?

While I was wrestling with those questions, something happened that served as a wake-up call. I came home late one night after Heidi had once again been left alone with the children. The boys were in bed, and she was finishing the dishes. She reached up to place a coffee mug on a high shelf, and it slipped out of her hand and hit the bottom shelf and shattered, cutting her arm. I helped her stop the bleeding, and as we were cleaning the wound, she burst into tears.

They weren't tears of physical pain; they were tears of frustration, tears that are wept after a long day and a sleepless night. Tears that are reminders that it all starts again in the morning. At that moment I saw the woman I said I loved in need of me. I realized her pain and frustration, and I sensed I was supposed to be there as her partner to share in her pain. That's what love does. I got Heidi into bed, and I went off and knelt on my knees and asked the Lord to change my heart and help me love and serve my wife with the same fervor that I had loved and served Him.

I began to see the truth that had been staring me in the face all along. Heidi was an equal partner in ministry, not a support system for my ministry ventures. She was my life mate, not my assistant and cheerleader. I had left out half the equation about putting God first. Yes, Jesus said, "You must love the Lord your God with all your heart, all your soul, and all your mind. This is the first and greatest commandment." But then He went on to say: "A second is equally important: 'Love your neighbor as yourself '" (Matthew 22:37, 39).

I was trying to love and honor God by putting Him first, but I was failing to love and honor Heidi, who was my first neighbor. I was failing to realize the equal importance of both facets of this command. I could not love God unless I loved others. I wasn't putting God first at all in my life if I wasn't demonstrating my love for Him in how well I loved others, beginning with my own family.[32]

***

God is up to something in this age. He is alive and leading his true church to reorder priorities and disciple people to love like Jesus. And we believe he wants you to enjoy his love and deepen your love for your spouse to depths you never dreamed possible. As you continue on that journey, you become "mirrors that brightly reflect the glory of the Lord. And as the Spirit of the Lord works within us, we become more and more like him and reflect his glory even more" (2 Corinthians 3:18 NLT*).

That verse highlights what I believe is the most impactful thing I have learned about loving like Jesus: our love comes from the Holy Spirit. Unfortunately, I was so ingrained in my old ways of thinking and acting that I had to change some of the most basic ways of my thinking. As I look back over the past years, the one thing that had the greatest influence on me was developing the simple habit of starting each day from the moment I wake up with the spoken question, "Coach, what are we going to change today?" By starting my day looking for change, I put myself in a receptive mindset for God to bring about a Christlike transformation. I am living proof that by looking for change from the beginning of the day, I am more receptive to the leading of the Spirit all day long.

Become part of this "Love Like Jesus" movement that we pray will continue to sweep this country and spread around the world. In the back of this book, you will find Called 2 Love courses and steps that will help lead you and your group to experience personally some of the principles and relational truths that Barbara and I continue to experience. They can help you launch a "Love Like Jesus" initiative in your own group and/or church.

A fitting close to this book is a prayer the apostle Paul made for Jesus' church. It is a prayer that Barbara and I pray for each of you as you continue your journey to know one another deeply with a heart of relational discovery:

> I pray that from his glorious, unlimited
> resources he will give you mighty inner
> strength through his Holy Spirit. And I
> pray that Christ will be more and more at
> home in your hearts as you trust in him.
> May your roots go down deep into the soil
> of God's marvelous love. And may you
> have the power to understand, as all God's
> people should, how wide, how long, how
> high, and how deep his love really is. May
> you experience the love of Christ, though it
> is so great you will never fully understand
> it. Then you will be filled with the fullness
> of life and power that comes from God.
> (Ephesians 3:16–21 NLT*)

APPENDIX

ABOUT THE GREAT COMMANDMENT NETWORK

The Great Commandment Network is an international collaborative network of strategic kingdom leaders from the faith community, marketplace, education, and caregiving fields who prioritize the powerful simplicity of the words of Jesus to love God, love others, and see others become His followers (Matthew 22:37–40, Matthew 28:19–20).

The Great Commandment Network is served through the following:

Relationship Press – This team collaborates, supports, and joins together with churches, denominational partners, and professional associates to develop, print, and produce resources that facilitate ongoing Great Commandment ministry.

The Center for Relational Leadership – Their mission is to teach, train, and mentor both ministry and corporate leaders in Great Commandment principles, seeking to equip leaders with relational skills so they might lead as Jesus led.

The Galatians 6:6 Retreat Ministry – This ministry offers a unique two-day retreat for ministers and their spouses for personal renewal and for reestablishing and affirming ministry and family priorities.

The Center for Relational Care (CRC) – The CRC provides therapy and support to relationships in crisis through an accelerated process of growth and healing, including Relational Care Intensives for couples, families, and singles.

For more information on how you, your church, ministry, denomination, or movement can be served by the Great Commandment Network write or call:

Great Commandment Network
2511 South Lakeline Blvd.
Cedar Park, Texas 78613
#800-881-8008

Or visit our website: GreatCommandment.net

Endnotes

1 "Post-Traumatic Stress Disorder," National Institute of Mental Health, February 2016, https://www.nimh.nih.gov/health/topics/post-traumatic-stress-disorder-ptsd/index.shtml.

2 Ibid.

3 Margery Williams, *The Velveteen Rabbit*, Project Gutenberg e-book #11757, 3, released in the public domain March 29, 2004, http://www.gutenberg.net/1/1/7/5/11757. The quotes from this eBook are for the use of anyone anywhere at no cost and with almost no restrictions whatsoever. You may copy these quotes, give them away, or re-use them under the terms of Project Gutenberg License included with these quotes from this eBook at www.gutenberg.net.

4 Ibid. 4.

5 Ibid. 10.

6 Courtesy of Linda Milner, Nsight Life Coaching, www.nsightlifecoaching.net.

7 Donald Miller, *Blue Like Jazz* (Nashville: Thomas Nelson Publishers, 2003), 64–76.

8 Josh McDowell with the Barna Group, *The Porn Phenomenon Study* (Ventura, CA: Barna Group, Ltd., 2016), 65, http://www.cbcrh.com/home/180005292/180009741/docs/The-Porn-Phenomenon.pdf?sec_id=180009741.

9 Ibid., 41.

10 Ibid., 81.

11 David and Teresa Ferguson, *Never Alone* (Austin, TX: Intimate Life Ministries, 2001), 152.

12 Joan Atwood, *The Effects of the Internet on Social Relationships: Therapeutic Considerations* (Bloomington, IN: iUniverse, 2011), 165–66.

13 Ibid.

14 Darryl DelHousaye, *The Primacy of Our Faith* (Scottsdale, AZ.: LLJ Ministries, 2017), 90.

15 Gaylord Enns, *Love Revolution* (Chico, CA: Love Revolution Press, 2011), 50–51, 60, used by permission of the author.

16 Jill Bolte Taylor, "My Stroke of Insight," TED Talk, February 2008, https://www.ted.com/talks/jill_bolte_taylor_s_powerful_stroke_of_insight.

17 Nora D. Volkow, MD, "Challenges and Opportunities in Drug Addiction Research: A Decade after The Decade of the Brain," February 18, 2010, http://dana.org/Cerebrum/2010/A_Decade_after_The_Decade_of_the_Brain__Challenges_and_Opportunities_in_Drug_Addiction_Research/.

18 Melanie Curtin, "This 75-Year Harvard Study Found the 1 Secret to Leading a Fulfilling Life," *Inc.*, February 27, 2017, https://www.inc.com/melanie-curtin/want-a-life-of-fulfillment-a-75-year-harvard-study-says-to-prioritize-this-one-t.html.

19 Ibid., emphasis added.

20 Mike McManus, "The Scandal of Southern Baptist Divorce," *Virtue Online*, July 7, 2010, http://www.virtueonline.org/scandal-southern-baptist-divorce-mike-mcmanus.

21 Barna Group, *New Research on the State of Discipleship* (Ventura, CA: Barna Group, Ltd., 2015), 2, https://www.barna.com/research/new-research-on-the-state-of-discipleship/.

22 Ibid., 3.

23 Ibid., 9.

24 Barna Group, *Many Church Goers and Faith Leaders Struggle to Define Spiritual Maturity* (Ventura, CA: Barna Group, Ltd., 2009), 1, 3, https://www.barna.com/research/many-churchgoers-and-faith-leaders-struggle-to-define-spiritual-maturity/.

25 Ibid.

26 Willow Creek Association, *Focus* (Barrington, IL: Willow Creek Resources, 2009), 104.

27 Ibid., 17.

28 Willow Creek Association, *Follow Me* (Barrington, IL: Willow Creek Resources, 2008), 108.

29 David Ferguson, *The Never Alone Church* (Cedar Park, TX.: Relational Press, 2016), 111–14.

30 Josh McDowell, *10 Ways to Say I Love You* (Eugene, OR: Harvest House Publishers, 2015), 20–21.

31 Gary Chapman and Harold Myra, *Married and Still Loving It* (Chicago: Moody Publishers, 2016), 155, 159.

32 Jeff Bogue, *Living Naked* (Akron, OH: Living Naked Press, 2009), 92–99.

With Deep Appreciation

We sit back in amazement and gratefulness when we reflect on how God has brought us through our own marriage journey. We are a testimony of what God can do in a relationship when a couple is open to change. Looking back, it's hard to imagine that sincerely focusing on Jesus' commandment to "love one another as I have loved you" would make such an amazing transformation in our lives, let alone let us see our transformed relationship published in a book.

There are so many people to recognize and thank for their valuable contribution to our lives and to this book:

Our daughters, Pam and husband Dan, and Tracy and husband Dave, for their undying love and support even though we brought unnecessary pain in their early years through our family dysfunctional behavior patterns.

Dave Bellis for collaborating with us on the book and writing the first draft. And to Tom Williams for reworking the manuscript of our true-life story to make it read more like a novel.

And again, thank you, Dave, for leading us into a strategic partnership with David Ferguson and the Great Commandment Network. One book has turned into three books, a six-week course, a national Called 2 Love Date Night tour, and much more. For more information, go to Called2Love.com.

Don Enevoldsen and his wife, Christina, who originally pored over reams of journals and hours of interviews with us to create the very first written version of our story. Don's manuscript laid the perfect foundation for what has come to pass.

Linda Milner for her insights, gifted counseling, patience, and kindness as she guided both of us to discover who we were and how to experience a greater emotional and relational healing.

Darryl DelHousaye, our former pastor, now Chancellor of Phoenix Seminary, and his wife, Holly, for walking with us through the entire Change Project and The Agape Project, launching us on the journey of Jesus' command to love one another as He loves us.

The Agape Project was the predecessor to the Called 2 Love Initiative. Thank you to Pastors Jamie Rasmussen and Tyler Johnson for the many hours they invested not only in our lives but also in how the message of relationally loving like Jesus could radically affect the church. And to Jason Lehman, a great friend, so dedicated to this reality and living it out in their family through three generations. We would also like to thank Ben Bost and Kent DelHousaye, who took a concept of the Agape Project and created the Love and Transformation Institute.

Our Scottsdale Team of Nicole Asmus, Amy Witsoe, and Marilyn Smock for their faithful support, loving hearts, and hard work in the effort to call people to love others as Jesus loves us.

David Ferguson, Terri Snead, and the Austin Great Commandment Team for adopting us into their ministry family and launching Called 2 Love. To BroadStreet Publishing Senior Editor Bill Watkins for his leadership and guidance. Also, to Christy Distler for her excellent editing and to the entire Broad-

Street team for their vision to get the message of Called 2 Love out to as many people and churches as possible.

I know we'll be embarrassed by missing someone, and we are truly sorry and thank you for your encouragement and support. But finally, to the one who knows us best and loves us most—Jesus himself. Without his loving us first, we would not know how to truly love at all. Words cannot express the depth of gratitude we have for our Savior and Lord, and for not only calling us to love like him, but for empowering us to make his love a living reality in our lives.

About the Authors

Steve and Barbara Uhlmann are the founders of and the heartbeat behind the Agape Project, LoveLikeJesus.com, The Intentional Community, and the Called 2 Love Initiative. After a financially successful career in the global plastics industry, Steve and Barbara came to the realization that they were married yet emotionally alone. Ghosts from the past and a health crisis in the present could have marked the end of it all. Instead, it denoted a new and wonderful beginning. Their journey from emotional woundedness to wholeness shows all of us how we can experience an ongoing relational intimacy with the one we love. The Uhlmanns have two adult children, six grandchildren, and three great grandchildren. They reside in Scottsdale, Arizona.

Engage with the Called 2 Love Movement:

- **In your family . . .** as loving your nearest ones becomes a top priority in imparting faith, to next generations.

- **In your church . . .** As a mentor couple, small group leader, or workshop presenter, living out Christ's new Commandment to love one another and help others to do the same (John 13:34).

- **In your community . . .** as being Called2Love like Jesus transforms families, neighborhoods, schools, and the marketplace.

- **As a church . . .** where the powerful simplicity of Great Commission Living Empowered by Great Commandment Love takes any church to the next level of Kingdom impact (Matthew 28:19-20, 22:37-40).

Visit *Called2Love.com/Journey* **to find out more!**

More Called 2 Love Resources

Order at: ***GreatCommandment.net/books***

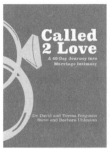

Called 2 Love
A 40-Day Journey into Marriage Intimacy

Using the power of story, the authors lead couples along their own journey to better know and care for each other. An excellent resource for couple mentoring, small groups and premarital counseling.

Called 2 Love
Like Jesus

An anthology of teachings and practical exercises from notable followers of Jesus.

Explore the transforming power of your call to love, *"as you have been loved."* Also included are practical disciplines to deepen your love of the Lord followed by loving family, friends, and those who need Jesus.

Called 2 Love
The Uhlmann Story

One couple's journey from a mere existence to deepened marriage intimacy.

Married for more than 50 years, Steve and Barbara continue to see relationships as the way to reveal Jesus to the people around us. In their new book, *Called2Love: The Uhlmann Story*, they share the principles of love and change that transformed their lives.

Another Relationship Resource

Can Christians reclaim sexuality in a broken culture? We say yes. *Rethinking Sexuality* challenges the paradigm of how Christians have traditionally approached conversations and questions about sexuality. *Rethinking Sexuality* is not just a book, but a movement to equip the Church in addressing biblical sexuality.

- Understand how every sexual question is ultimately a spiritual one
- View sexuality not as a problem to solve but as a territory to reclaim
- See how sexuality is rooted in the broader context of God's heart for us
- Grasp the bigger picture of sexual challenges and wholeness
- Shift the challenge from combating sexual problems to proclaiming and modeling sacred sexuality

Visit: authenticintimacy.com/rethinking to order and to receive a free sample chapter.